THE SCHOOL LEAVER'S GUIDE TO MONEY

£

WRITTEN BY

RAY SPOONER

First published in Great Britain as a softback original in 2021

Copyright © Ray Spooner

The moral right of this author has been asserted.

Typeset in Athelas

Editing, design, typesetting and publishing by UK Book Publishing

www.ukbookpublishing.com

ISBN: 978-1-914195-74-7

For my Grandchildren Harry, Teddy, George and Lily and all those yet to be born. I love you all. May you live a life of freedom.

THE SCHOOL LEAVER'S GUIDE TO MONEY

CONTENTS

PREFACE

I'm probably what people would call a working-class boy made good. I was born in the East End of London, the last of the true Cockneys.

Until the age of seven I lived in a two-up two-down mid-terraced council house in Bow, with an outside toilet. We used to bathe in a tin bath my mum used to carry in from the yard.

They knocked down our terraces and built high-rise buildings in the late sixties and the council rehoused us to Dagenham. I remember pulling up at our new house, which had an inside toilet and three bedrooms, in disbelief. We couldn't believe our luck.

My schooling was at the local comprehensive where university was rarely if ever mentioned and only a handful of us made it to university. It was a tough school and most people came out with a handful of O Levels and went into some sort of manual job at the age of 16.

I was lucky enough to be taken on as an engineering apprentice. Apprenticeships were common in those days and so were jobs.

I lasted seven years at that firm confined to four factory walls and eventually when I could take no more, I left my well-paid engineering career behind. I started at the bottom again, labouring in the building industry, digging trenches at the age of 23, with not much to show for my seven years at work.

I wanted to share my little trip down memory lane with you because I want you to be confident that wherever you are in life right now, you can build a good level of wealth, it's not beyond your capability. It is not about your level of education or how much money you earn, it's about the direction you want to take in life and what you want to achieve.

I wrote this book to help you on your journey. To open up your mind to an alternative route to wealth that you may not have considered before, or even known existed.

I will be sharing my knowledge and experience of the last 36 years in business, education and investing. My intention is to give you a set of skills that will help you understand how to use money like the rich have been doing for thousands of years. Then if you wish, to use those new skills to build wealth. You will certainly not be given that knowledge at school or university.

I'm sure you can appreciate that my journey from the beginning to where I am today, took a lot of hard work and required me to take a great deal of action, some of which was well outside of my comfort zone. It will be the same for you should you choose this route, but the rewards of time and money at a relatively young age will be well worth it.

Becoming wealthy has not been a quick process for me. Going from where I started, to understanding what I needed to do to accrue wealth, took many years. I feel my slow start was due to the conditioning I'd received from everything around me, school, the media, even my friends and family.

I was in my forties when I finally had the lightbulb moment and really learned how to use money, and my god did it change my life. Even at that age I was able to accrue a good level of wealth in only a few years. Just think what you can do at your age.

The same knowledge I learned is now making my five sons wealthy. They were very young when they learned the skills in this book and will be financially independent well before I was. The point here is the earlier you start, the younger you will be when you are financially free.

That said, this isn't a get-rich-quick book. I don't believe that is possible. This is a get rich slow and steady book, building genuine wealth based on appreciating assets. This book is really about changing your lifestyle to include good financial habits.

The book has been in my thoughts for several years, and the recent global pandemic and the economic disaster that will follow have prompted me to get my thoughts down on paper quickly, so that it may give you some direction in life in this uncertain time.

This is my second book, my first being about how to start and build a business. It took months to write specifically to help young people learn what they should have learned in school, to get a Wealth Mind-Set.

Plain English

Some of the topics in this book are fairly complex. But don't worry, I've been careful to explain them in simple terms and I've used plain English, keeping away from jargon – and there's a lot in the financial industry.

The information in this book is the result of dealing with the finances of various businesses over a 37-year period and many thousands of hours in study. The book is meant to be a good overview of the subjects and not a detailed work; however, throughout the book I direct you to other books that delve deeper and have been invaluable to my learning.

By the end of the book you will have the skills to start changing your financial future, working toward substantial wealth if you so wish.

Disclaimer

The information in this book is my opinion only and cannot be taken as financial, investment or any other advice. It represents my personal experience.

ABOUT

....

This book is to teach young people how to use money wisely to become financially free

The skills I share with you in this book are what has given me the lifestyle I want, free time and passive income to enable me to enjoy life, free from money worries. These skills are now doing the same for my sons.

My 23-year old Luke has planned to be financially free by the time he is 35. My 19-year-old Alex even earlier; and I have written here exactly how they are doing it and how my five sons and I are doing it as a family.

By the time you have completed the book you will know more about how to use money than most of the population. I hope you use this knowledge to your advantage, because a life with limited money is a hard and stressful life.

It seems much of the population have money worries and is it any wonder. How many people take the time to study money or even realise there is such a subject. All it takes, like most things, is prioritising the time. Sadly, most people haven't the inclination.

If you asked the people you know the actual steps they would take to become wealthy, I'd bet not many would know where to start. You, on the other hand after reading this book, will know exactly where to start. You will have all the skills you need, a detailed formula for wealth.

But like anything in life worth having, there will be a price to pay. You will have to prioritise some of your time and take action on the Skills on a daily basis and dedicate your life to this endeavour.

You will need to be very strong minded to pull this off. Everything around you will be pulling you away from your goal, so you must think for yourself. Do not accept what the education system, all mainstream media and the government have told you all your life, because they do not have your best interests at heart, and it is very important that you begin to recognise this.

I'm hoping the fact that you bought this book means that you are serious about changing your financial future. You have taken the first step of your financial journey to improve yours and your family's life forever.

Who is the book for?

This book is for you if you:

- Want to know how to become financially free.
- Want to have more time to do as you please.
- Want to understand how to invest money to protect your loved ones.
- Want to pass on good money skills to your children.
- Want to leave a legacy for your children.
- Value freedom.

If you could have chosen the best time in history to read this book, now would probably be it.

At the time of writing in 2021 we are in the middle of the Covid-19 pandemic and the most unbelievable government control of human beings in history. The damage this is going to do to small businesses and the economy will change people's lives forever. The national and the global monetary system is going to look very different in the near future.

Whether you believe in the mainstream media or the alternative media narrative of why this is happening to us, one thing is for sure: our financial futures are very uncertain. This is a great time to know more about money and how to protect yourself and your family.

How the book is structured

For ease of reference, I've structured the book into 30 Skills. The skills are set within five Parts plus a Bonus Section. Parts 1, 2 and 3 give you the background on our money and banking system, the brief history of money and the kind of mind-set you'll need to become financially free.

In parts 4 and 5, I give you the actual skills you need to start your wealth journey.

In the Bonus Section I cover the skills you will need to buy or rent a home, buy a car, open a bank account and discuss credit scores and how incredibly important they are to you.

The Parts in summary:

Part 1. The wealth mind-set

In Part 1 I set the scene with a discussion on why school and college taught us nothing about money and why the system was specifically designed that way.

I go on to give you the most important knowledge, the wealth mindset which underpins the skills in this book. This will introduce you to a different way of thinking about money and life, so you can begin to design your future.

Part 2. What is money?

Part 2 is really background knowledge, preparing you for the hard-financial skills later in Parts 4 and 5. Here we discover that what we think of as money is actually currency. I explain the difference between currency and money, and discuss the meaning of 'real money' and why this is so important to you.

Every 75 years or so there has been a financial reset resulting in a different currency, and it is 75 years since the last one. What will come next is anyone's guess, but I will talk about the front runners for the new currency, so you can be prepared.

Part 3. The banking system

Here again I am preparing you for Parts 4 and 5. In order to understand money, you have to understand the banking system and how it operates alongside governments.

We will discover how bankers and those who own the banks have been robbing the public for hundreds of years and many feel the entire system is fraudulent. I go on to discuss how you can protect your money from this broken system.

Part 4. Wealth knowledge

Here we deep-dive into the specific financial principles you will need to accrue wealth and become an investor. With a discussion on passive income and assets and liabilities. I also give you an example of how you can achieve financial freedom in only 15-20 years on a low income.

Part 5. Investing

Investing is often seen by the masses as something other people do. The perception is that it is complicated and risky. In truth, it's far from complicated and doesn't have to be risky. Anyone can do it.

I will talk you through the main types of investment class and how you can get started. I discuss property investing, buying land, gold and silver, stocks and shares and digital currencies such as Bitcoin, and show you how easy it is to enter these markets.

Bonus Section. Money essentials for life

With the main body behind us, we take a look at the various financial transactions you could be involved with at some stage. For example, you will probably need to open a bank account, buy a car, and rent or buy a house. I've given you some insider tips I've learned along the way which will save you money and help you deal with the sales people.

I also discuss credit and credit scores and why a good score is critical to your financial future.

COVID-19

I started writing this book in 2019 and then guess what? Covid happened and threw a spanner in the works. I wasn't sure how to handle it at first; do I rewrite sections to reflect how things are in the pandemic, or do I carry on as if nothing has happened.

As time went by I realised that some of the topics I'd written about had changed – mainly the ones that require human interaction, like buying a car or viewing a house, at least temporarily.

After some thought I felt the worst thing to do would be to ignore the subject as I felt this would be disrespectful to you, the reader. I decided to inform you, reader, how I'd dealt with writing the book at this time.

I scanned the content of my book for areas that would be dealt with slightly differently due to Covid. I felt the concepts discussed up to Skill 23 would not change.

Some of Skills 23-30 could be affected, in that the human contact involved in buying a car for example, or viewing a house, would be more on-line and less fact-to-face.

However, I have found many estate agents are still carrying out viewings in person and many car dealers are allowing people to visit their showroom, as I found when I bought a car recently. In fact, there seems to be no norms and it appears to be that each company is interpreting the guidelines differently. Therefore, I have concluded it is impossible here to cover all the variables.

I am asking the reader to take the content of this book and realise that some interactions may change, hopefully temporarily, until the pandemic is finally over.

Now let's get into Part 1. Let me enlighten you as to why they didn't teach us about money at school. Please keep an open mind.

PART I:
THE WEALTH MIND-SET

A note on wealth

Throughout the book I mention the word 'wealth', but realise that wealth means different things to different people. To a billionaire a millionaire could appear poor.

To me, wealth means more than just money; it also means health, happiness and freedom.

But since the book is about money, when I refer to wealth I refer to:

Having enough money to do what you want, when you want, without having to work. With no financial worries.

The Skills in this section are:

1. Why they didn't teach me about money at school.
2. What they didn't teach me about work at school.
3. Changing to a Wealth Mind-Set.

SKILL I:
WHY THEY DIDN'T TEACH ME ABOUT MONEY AT SCHOOL

"A child educated only at school is an uneducated child."
George Santayana

I don't know about you, but in all my years in education I can honestly say no teacher ever taught me how to use money to become wealthy. Therefore, it seems fair to ask, why not? Why did the people who designed the syllabus feel it not important to pass on one of the main life skills we are all going to need?

One answer is that our teachers don't know how to use money themselves. How many rich teachers do you know?

The logical conclusion has to be, that the education system must have been designed specifically 'not' to teach you about money, and many experts believe this to be case.

I didn't give this a second thought at school; we don't, do we, we just turn up and listen to what the teacher has to say without question. It's only when we leave school, we realise we have limited money skills and are totally unprepared for many areas of adult life. Or maybe like most people we don't even realise then, and this could be why most people are blissfully ignorant about money all their lives.

I picked up the basics, like buying a car and getting a mortgage (See Bonus Section) from my parents and friends, who had some idea of what they were doing. But anything deeper than that, like investing or how to get passive income, and they were as ignorant as I was. It's understandable: they were educated in the same system as you and me.

This is how entire families stay relatively poor for generations, locked into the same education system, followed by the work system that throws them out at retirement age with a few years left to enjoy.

My parents were products of that system and through no fault of their own, passed that way of thinking down to me. But somehow, probably through reading, almost by chance I slowly became consciously aware of what was really going on in the world.

I can only give you an idea here as to why school teaches us nothing about money, but for further reading please get a copy of *Weapons of Mass Instruction*, by John Taylor Gatto. Also *Dumbing Us Down* by John Taylor Gatto. They are an eye-opening read.

In his books, Gatto explains how the General Education Board, GEB, was set up by John D. Rockefeller in 1903. This was a completely new education system and the syllabus was controlled by Rockefeller. This became the model for the global education system and was apparently designed to turn-out loyal, non-thinking, obedient workers for the Rockefellers and other elites growing global businesses.

Also in 1901, Frederick Taylor Gates designed the Rockefeller Institute for Medical Research on behalf of John D Rockefeller. This was the beginning of the shift away from natural remedies that had been in existence for thousands of years. The beginning of the pharmaceutical drug-fuelled medical industry we know today. Today, Big Pharma is one the most lucrative industries on the planet.

The term 'quack' came from Rockefeller propaganda, meaning a doctor who practises natural remedies.

A Google search will flag-up that all this was done in the name of philanthropy by Rockefeller, but make no mistake: this was self-interest and control of the masses on a global scale.

Gatto explains how the education system is really a system of forced schooling or programming based on learning by memory, habit training and conformance. The top students in our system are those who can memorise facts, as can be seen by our examination system. Not the ones who have the ability to think creatively or critically. Many of the great names of the recent past such as Steve Jobs and the like did not go to university, or dropped out.

A good example is what is going on in the world right now. At this time, February 2021, most of the population are wearing a face mask as instructed by the government. This may or may not be a good idea, but how many of us have reviewed the scientific data and made up our own mind? Most of us listen to the news assuming what the nice person in the suit is telling us is the truth. Our compliance training at school has ensured that we are good compliant citizens.

You should also consider that what you have been taught at school is not necessarily accurate, but someone else's version of history, the version that certain people want you to know. But is it really the truth? Google and YouTube have recently been removing large amounts of content that does not agree with the mainstream narrative. That is creating a one-sided version of history.

As researcher James Corbett of the Corbett Report suggests, this has been done many times throughout history. The fire at the Great Library of Alexandria over 2000 years ago is a good example. The works of Socrates, Homer and Plato were destroyed, which wiped out some of the greatest works in history. More recently by Nazi Germany – the Nazi book burnings were a campaign to burn any books that did not agree with the narrative of the Nazi party.

Gatto explains that School also instils in us a sense of obedience to official directions. For example, "Miss can I use the toilet please?"

or, "your homework has to be in by this time". Many experts feel this is designed to prepare us for a life of agreeable subservience later in the workplace and to other authority such as the government, police or medical staff.

What our education system doesn't teach you is to question anything, when in fact you should question everything. Think for yourself, be creative, think critically and take responsibility. These are the traits which will help you achieve success and lead to a good life.

A deeper understanding of the above is really the starting point to your future wealth, as your eyes will begin to open to how, not only the education system but the world, is run. This entrepreneurial attitude will help enormously later when you begin investing.

To uni or not to uni, that is the question

In the early 2000s, the government was encouraging schools to be run more like businesses. I was approached and asked to mentor a head teacher in this regard, which ended up being for a couple of years.

With every visit I disliked what I saw more. I learned that head teachers mostly care about one thing: how many A-C grades their students get. The school's teaching efforts were mainly put into the 'Joe average 80%' with a view to upping the overall grades. The top and bottom 10% were treated as second class citizens. Better GCSE grades meant a better league table position. This meant more students applied to the school, which meant the school got more funding, and this is the end goal of a head teacher: growth of the school.

Schools are just like businesses, and you are just the product of the factory. I found that very alarming at the time and not a lot has changed.

This factory continues into the university system. We need to understand that the whole system is a great big money-making machine, taking more than £9,000 a year from the tax payer per student. With the support of massive mainstream media brainwashing over decades, parents see their kids going to UNI as a badge of honour. When in fact it is not appropriate for many young people who, like me, are practical learners not academics, and struggle in the university system.

It seems to be engrained in our culture to want our kids to go to university these days, and I've found any discussion to the contrary to be fairly controversial.

The fact is that even if you come out of university with a great paying job and work as a high-income earner for the rest of your life, it is very doubtful if you will ever be able to build the sort of wealth I am going to teach you to build in this book. There is a big difference between a high-income earner and someone who has the knowledge to build serious wealth.

By the end of this book you will be armed with more knowledge to decide whether to go to university or choose an alternative route.

I'll say up-front that I am biased, as none of my five sons went to university, and neither did I.

Let's take a look at some of the pros and cons of going to UNI, first from a money perspective.

If you decide to start work at age 16-17 in an apprenticeship, instead of sixth form college, the money situation could look something like this:

Work route

Year 1. Age 17. Apprentice	£9,300
Year 2. Age 18. Apprentice	£10,000
Year 3. Age 19. Trainee	£15,000
Year 4. Age 20. Trainee	£17,000
Year 5. Age 21. Improver	£20,000

Money earning potential £71,300

University route

Year 1. Age 17. Sixth form college Parent funded.	£?
Year 2. Age 18. Sixth form college Parent funded.	£?
Year 3. Age 19. Tuition + Living	-£15,000
Year 4. Age 20. Tuition + Living	-£15,000
Year 5. Age 21 Tuition + Living	-£15,000

Total cost -£45,000

If you go to university you could come out with around £45,000 worth of debt to be paid back later in life when you start earning £27,295 a year.

If you look around and are lucky enough to get on an apprenticeship you could earn more than £71,000 over the same five-year period. Even if you go to sixth form and miss UNI you will still walk away with over £52,000. That's a massive head start in life. If you invested that money into buying a rental property, it would pay you over £500 a month for the rest of your life. I shall write about this in more detail in Skill 16 and 19.

From a money perspective, there is no doubt that in the short-term, you will be much better off. Still, many young people decide to go regardless of the money. What, then, is the argument for university?

As far as I can tell, there seems to be two main arguments put forward for going to university. These are that you can get a better job earning more money. Also, that the experience will teach you to be independent.

Argument 1. Better job with more money.

It may be true that you could get a higher paying job with a degree, but that is far from guaranteed. I know some young people who have a degree and are working in a supermarket or a shop, earning just above minimum wage.

If you are lucky enough to get a job when you leave UNI, it will probably be a trainee role earning not much over £20,000 for a few years before you see the benefits of a higher wage. You will be in your mid-twenties by then and those who went from school into the workplace could have been promoted and will have a considerable financial advantage over you, which will be hard to make up.

But let's say you do leave UNI and land your perfect job as say, a solicitor. Apart from being a trainee for some years after UNI, you will spend a large amount of your life cooped-up in a small office, surrounded by mounds of paper. If this is your idea of fun, then great; it's certainly not mine.

My solicitor, for example, spends much of his life in the above situation and I often have to call him to chase him up when I'm completing on property deals. He always sounds stressed. I'm supposed to be the uneducated one, yet who is working for whom? It's a similar situation with my accountant, bank manager, dentist, and actuary, who looks after my pension funds.

From what I can tell, people in those types of professions have little freedom unless they run their own practices and have staff to do the day-to-day for them. But most are told what to do and when to do it.

Admittedly, most of these folks are on a higher wage, but many are under a great deal of pressure to appear successful to their peers and the public whom they serve. Who would want to go see an accountant or solicitor who drives an old banger and lives in a bad area? They have to have nice suits, good cars and homes to keep up with their peers. All this comes at a price and many I have known have been big consumers with not much spare cash or investments; they spend what they earn. As we will see in Skill 3, this will greatly hinder your chances of becoming financially free. They are also very time poor, often working long hours.

Of course, the above are generalisations, but usually it is only the business owners who get the money and the freedom.

I totally get that there are people who are driven towards a particular vocation. Maybe you want to be a scientist or a medical practitioner and that's fine. University may be the only route to achieve your dream. But as long as you go in with your eyes open and understand what I've discussed above.

Argument 2. The experience will teach you to be independent.

You often hear parents justify why their son or daughter went to UNI by saying, "it will be a good experience for them, it will make them independent".

But correct me if I'm wrong, being independent means not only being able to look after yourself, but being able to pay for yourself. In fact, without money how can you look after yourself?

Maybe you could argue that the experience of meeting young people from all over is a good thing and character building. At the same time, starting a new job at the age of 16 or 17 could be even more character building, forcing you out of your comfort zone and accepting more responsibility.

The people you meet during UNI would be predominantly of a similar age group and this could be a disadvantage. People you will meet in the workplace will be mixed age groups, which will reflect the interactions in society and your future working life, and so could be more beneficial to your social development.

At the end of the day, it is your choice whether you go to UNI or not. But it must be your choice, not someone else's, and certainly not just because that's what everyone else does.

One young guy, Adam, who works for our company, told me he had to go to Uni. He was the first person in his family who ever had the chance to go. His grandparents and parents were egging him on and he got carried away with the thought of how proud they would be of him, rather than what he wanted himself.

He said the whole three years was a waste of time and that he'd learned more in the first three months at work than the entire three years at Uni.

I feel this is a common story and I would urge you to consider your long-term future when making your decision. It is 'your' decision, not your parents'.

SKILL 2:
WHAT THEY DIDN'T TEACH ME
ABOUT WORK AT SCHOOL

Some of what I'm about to say could come across a little harsh to some people, but like any good parent should do, I'm here to tell you the truth to help you build a good life. Sometimes that requires a little tough love.

When I was at school we had a subject called Careers. The careers department consisted of one lady in a tiny shoe box office who you visited once and were asked the question, "What do you want to do when you leave school?". That was about the extent of the knowledge we were given about the workplace. Looking back, I realise it was pathetic, and just showed the importance school placed on our future careers.

Having been an employer myself now for over 30 years, I know what makes a good employee and if I were a careers teacher, my students would leave school or university with the inside story on how to act and achieve in the workplace, and with a detailed knowledge of all the main jobs. But alas, even today young people leave with very little knowledge of the workplace. I know this for a fact having employed many school leavers over the years.

Most people we employ have no idea what the boss 'really' wants from their employees and how they can achieve in the workplace.

They are under the misconception that it is all about being good at the job; it is not. From an employer's perspective, many other things are also important.

Let me go through what they should have told you at school. What to do in the workplace to get promoted and given a pay rise quickly. You just have to understand how the game works and the most important part of the game is good attitude.

Good attitude

Most of us won't be able to start the journey of wealth accumulation until we start work and get paid. How well we get on at work, and how much we earn, will depend to a great extent on our attitude.

Let me define what I mean by good attitude. Good attitude in the workplace means: putting yourself out to be helpful. It's not difficult and I bet if more people knew how important this was to an employer, they'd put themselves out to be more helpful.

You need the right attitude at work from day one. I would go so far as to say that good attitude is the most important trait, even more so than being good at your job.

An example of people with good attitudes are two young guys we have in our business. They both started with us from UNI in admin. But, as the business has grown, we have needed them to help out in other departments. They have always been willing to help and in the process their skills are developing as they learn more of the business. They are both friendly and happily help-out with whatever the business needs them to do with a smile. They are a pleasure to have around and the firm would do anything to keep them employed.

Poor attitude

Unfortunately, we have found in our business that many people have a poor attitude, some even have an entitled attitude. Not wanting to do the menial tasks like make a cup of tea or take the bins out, thinking this is below them. Some refuse to help a colleague in a different department because, "it isn't my job".

I've found that some youngsters we employ seem to want everything, now, and are simply not willing to start at the bottom and work their way up the ladder, like people from previous generations took for granted.

The hard truth is that anyone with poor attitude who thinks the world owes them a living, will find it hard to keep a job, let alone become wealthy, because in the workplace you are expected to be helpful and pull your weight, or you will be fired.

It always shocks me that when you do sack someone who has a bad attitude that they seem surprised. Maybe they have been allowed to get away with that in other areas of their lives, but not at work. Of course they are going to be fired, it's just a matter of time.

Unlike your parents, the workplace will not nurture and love you. It will not protect you from the harsh realities of life, or take responsibility for the things you should be doing. On the contrary, it won't care much for you at all. It cares mainly about one thing: how much money you can make the business. From this point on you need to unlearn most of what you have learned in the education system, which knows little about the workplace, and align yourself with the realities of work.

Holding down a job is surprisingly less to do with ability and more to do with turning up on time, being polite and doing what you are asked to do, and I mean anything, and be pleased to do it. If you do this, from my experience as an employer, you will already be light-years ahead of the competition.

In the past, we have had one lady leave because I asked her to make a cup of tea. One because we asked her to help out in the buying department, saying it wasn't her job. Another left the same day because she didn't realise there was so much work to do, throwing away a three-year apprenticeship. I could go on, but I think you get the picture. Do not be that person.

Employee types:

As an employer, I've employed hundreds of people over the years and have found, with little exception, three types of people. See if you can spot yourself from the list below. The type you are will affect the way the company perceives you and remunerates you. It will affect everything about your financial future and how long you are with the firm.

These are the three general types of people I've observed over the years:

- Average Ability with Good Attitude (Star)
- High Ability with Poor Attitude (Fallen Star)
- High Ability with Good Attitude (Super Star)

Star

If you are a person with average ability but a good attitude: you turn up on time every day and do what is asked of you, not wanting to accept much responsibility; you are a star. If you are at the bottom end of stardom, in that you are not that helpful, you will not be that highly thought of by the company.

In my experience, you will be like the vast majority of employees and from the firm's perspective you will probably be seen as a resource fulfilling a role the firm needs doing at that time, but will probably be among the first to be let go if the firm gets short of work, as there are lots of people like you around. That said, the better your attitude and the more helpful you are, the more you'll be thought of by the company. Some stars are with companies for many years.

I have found Stars to be nice, hard-working people, generally with no ambition who are content to turn-up and do their job. The company needs folks like this to carry out routine tasks, but they will never be paid much above industry rates or rise-up through the ranks. In my experience, the majority of the workforce fits into this category.

My feeling on what holds them back is their lack of ability to cope with responsibility, and they therefore seek-out low responsibility, high repetition tasks within their comfort zone.

My advice if you feel you fit in this category, is be helpful. Become invaluable to the company and make sure you have a very good attitude. If so, you will be kept in employment and given pay rises when other less helpful stars are let go.

Fallen stars

Some people are talented but with a poor attitude. I have found these people to be particularly difficult to deal with over the years; intelligence mixed with a willingness to disrupt isn't a good combination for a company.

These people often seem great to an employer at first, as they pick up the job quickly, say all the right things and earn the firm money. But, after the honeymoon period ends, their bad attitude begins to shine through. This can range from just poor attitude to downright disruptive behaviour.

I've worked with some people who are very talented and, as an employer, have tended to put up with bad attitude for a while because they are so good at their job. But invariably the attitude becomes too much to deal with or other employees become disgruntled, or they even upset clients, and you have to let them go; preferably sooner rather than later.

Super star

Now if you work really hard or are one of the lucky people, you will be what I call a Super Star and the world will be yours, my friend.

Some people I have worked with, albeit not many, have both good attitude and a lot of ability. These are the people who get promoted quickly and paid more than their peers.

The firm will go to great lengths to keep you as it knows you will make more money for the company. If you recognise you are a Super Star, you should exploit it. Push for more money immediately, even if you've been with the firm a short while. Strike while the iron's hot as they say. If the firm sees you in this way, there is a very good chance that you will get the pay rise you want, as, trust me, the firm will not want to lose you; there are not many of you around. We have paid well over the going rate for these people.

Super Stars have certain abilities that others do not. Besides a natural affinity to the job, the main difference I have found between average employees and super stars, is their ability to take on responsibility and handle that without getting stressed. This is a rare trait indeed and if you have it you will probably have identified it in yourself from an early age. You will probably be the person who takes responsibility for confronting difficult situations where others shy away.

Some Super Stars are the sort of people who get to director level or sometimes start businesses of their own. Although this requires additional personal traits and other skillsets such as great people skills and the discipline to give up the time to develop themselves personally in all areas.

I have made the mistake of assuming someone is a Super Star, when in fact time has shown them to be a Fallen Star. If you are a Fallen Star masquerading as a Super Star, you will be found out in time. A person cannot disguise their values for long, their unconscious behaviour always shows through in the end.

How to do well in the workplace

Since holding down a job is vital to you becoming wealthy, let me please share with you from an employer's perspective how to do very well, very quickly at work.

One fact in our business is that all the poor attitude people get fired eventually, presumably going from firm to firm with that attitude. All the good ones have a job with us for as long as they want.

Alongside doing a good job, just be friendly and helpful, the most helpful person in the building (or out of the building at the present time). Offer to make the tea – it won't kill you – and do more than you are paid to do. I promise, it will come back to you in loyalty and financially a hundred times over.

This sounds so easy, and it is for a person with the right attitude, but for a person who thinks this stuff is below him or her, it's very difficult to swallow their pride to do such lowly tasks. Well, more fool you, you are thinking with your balls and not your brains as my old dad used to say.

But, when thinking with your brains it's easy to reverse the psychology. Realise that by accommodating the boss, you are not feathering his or her nest but your own. You are the one that will get the promotion and pay rise. You have to, you've made yourself invaluable to the firm and they will not want to lose you.

This will lead to more money, which will mean you will get to your financial freedom goal quicker. That's using your brains.

SKILL 3: CHANGING TO A WEALTH MIND-SET

So far, we've covered why school did not teach you about money and also how you can achieve in the workplace. Now let's move on to get your mind prepared for the exciting journey to financial independence.

I would say that this is the most important section of the book and underpins all the other skills. I'm going to encourage you to start thinking about money like the wealthy and lose your old spending habits.

From what I've seen, by far the majority of people in the UK do not know how to handle money, but certainly know how to spend it. Most are consumers with an earn-and-spend mentality driven by advertising. This is helping to keep them poor.

It took me many years to learn what I'm going to share with you here. Many of those years I have to say, I did have a good lifestyle from my business. But although I had money I still had to give up a lot of my time for the business to maintain my consumer lifestyle. It wasn't until I learned about passive income, income that comes in whether you are asleep or on a beach, that I really started to be successful.

If you are ready and willing to learn, I am going to give you a new approach which could make you wealthy.

THE FIRST RULE OF WEALTH:

WEALTHY PEOPLE BUY APPRECIATING ASSETS WHICH CAN GIVE THEM A RETURN.

POOR PEOPLE BUY DEPRECIATING LIABILITIES WHICH KEEPS THEM POOR.

Those are two of the most important lines you will ever read if your goal is financial freedom. But what do they mean?

Assets and Liabilities are discussed in detail in Skill 13, but are defined here:

An asset must be something:

- You own that maintains or goes up in value.
- You own that gives a return (income).
- You do not own that gives you a return (Skill 19).

A liability is something:

- That costs you money and goes down in value.

Let me illustrate the long-term effect on a person's life of buying assets compared to another person buying liabilities.

John

A life of spending

After university John got a job in a bank. His starting pay wasn't that great, but he felt he had good prospects.

John was the sort of guy who liked nice things. His taste for designer clothes grew in-line with his pay.

John was all about image, he wanted his friends and neighbours to think he was successful. As soon as he could drive he bought a flash car on finance. He couldn't really afford the repayments, but the thought of what his friends would think was stronger than the thought of getting into debt.

As time went by John became a high wage earner and was able to get a big mortgage. He had all the outward signs of wealth, nice cars, several holidays a year; anyone looking at John's lifestyle would assume he was doing very well.

But the monthly repayments on the mortgage, car and his credit card bills meant that whatever he earned he spent, and this left him very tight for cash each month.

The years went by and now in his early fifties he'd been working for the bank for 25 years. He was tired of the daily commute and began to value time over money.

The problem was that he had no savings or other forms of income other than his wage and although he'd enjoyed a good life, now in his mid-fifties he realised he may have to keep working well into his retirement years to maintain his current lifestyle. In reality, he had no choice.

Sam

A life of saving and investing

Sam initially went to university, but realised after a short while it wasn't for her. She was more of a practical type so left after only one term at age 18. She started working in a pub which she loved but was minimum wage. She'd always been the type to save her money and she put away as much as she could.

After a year she left her job and started at a new pub, this time in the restaurant, but again on a low wage. But she had the opportunity to earn tips which could be very lucrative. This enabled her to save even more.

As her experience grew so did her career and by her mid-twenties she was managing the restaurant of a large pub chain. The money was much better, and still living with her parents meant she could save half her wage.

She did go on holidays and had a basic car, but she lived a frugal life which enabled her to save £400 a month initially, then £600 as her wage increased.

By the time she was 24 she had more than £35,000 in the bank. She wanted to make that money grow and a friend told her about someone who had bought a buy-to-let rental property, which paid rent every month.

She went on a property course and eventually bought her first buy-to-let, putting down a deposit of £25,000, giving her an income of £400 a month after paying the mortgage.

She was promoted at work so could save even more. Within only two years she had enough money to buy another property.

Now she had £800 rental income per month totalling £9,600 per year.

It took a further two years to save another £15,000 to buy property three at the age of 28.

The rental income of three properties was a whopping £14,400 a year, and in only eighteen-months she was able to buy property four.

Sam got married during that year and luckily her new husband agreed with her frugal approach to life. Together they bought a further 12 houses before Sam was 40, giving them a net income of £76,800 per year, meaning that from the age of 40, neither of them ever had to work ever again.

But of course they did work, but on their terms. They chose when they worked and what sort of work they did, and had lots of time to spend with their children. By the time they were both 50 they had a passive income of more than £120,000 a year and the icing on the cake was that as well as the rental income, most of the properties had doubled in value since Sam first started buying.

The end.

The stories illustrate the end position in life of two people with different approaches to using money.

If you think I'm exaggerating, think again. My son Luke is 24, he has two properties already which bring him in nearly £11,000 a year, all paid for himself from his savings. He is in the process of looking for property number three.

Becoming wealthy is not some earth-shattering secret; the concept is simple. The tough part is having the courage, determination and persistence to live your life in accordance with the wealth mind-set philosophy and the drive to take action to make it happen. Most people cannot or do not want to put in either the time or the effort.

You can see from the above examples, that becoming wealthy does not depend on your age, wage or job, whether you are a man or woman; it's about one thing only: your spending and saving habits.

The compounded effect of Sam's early saving and investing lifestyle as opposed to John's consumer lifestyle made a massive difference to the quality of their lives over the long-term. In Skill 16, I map out the figures and time required for anyone to become financially free using investment property.

In fact, having a great job earning lots of money can be a disadvantage. High income earners like doctors or accountants are under a great deal of pressure to keep up appearances with their peers. Big houses and big cars are expensive. I call these people, rich poor people. They have all the outwards signs of wealth, but it's all based on debt.

At the end of the day, the determining factor of your wealth will be whether you are a consumer or an investor. It is the compounded effects of your spending habits over a long period that will determine whether you end up poor or wealthy.

Your get rich strategy is to quietly tuck away your money in your savings account consistently. Live frugally, do not buy stuff. Limit clothes, only buy the essentials of life. Don't have ten pairs of trainers, have two. Don't pay £4000 for a holiday, pay £700. Save save save until you have enough money to buy a rental property or any of the other investment strategies I will share with you in Part 5.

Anyone can do it and the younger you start the better, so don't waste your time going to university unless you want to commit your life to a particular calling or vocation. If your goal is freedom of time and money, follow my formula as soon as possible.

Don't listen to the naysayers

For most of you, the concepts you'll learn in this book will challenge the way you've been using money your entire life. When you start to change your habits for the better, you could get some negative comments especially from well-meaning family and friends. Those close to you seem to be the ones who are your biggest critics, with comments like, "enjoy yourself while you are young", or "you deserve a nice car you work hard". It's natural for us to go to those close to us for advice, but we have to ask ourselves, are they the best people to offer us the advice we need. Are they wealthy?

Choose carefully who you take advice from. Listen to people who can prove they have done what you want to do.

In the early days while you are saving enough money to invest, you will have to be incredibly strong minded. Those around you will likely have a consumer mind-set, buying all sorts of liabilities. You will have to be frugal buying only on a needs-basis and saving as much as you can as quickly as possible.

Financial education

When you start it could take up to five years to save enough for your first investment; this is by far the hardest part. Don't waste those years. Use the time to learn about money and how to invest. Use your initial saving years to develop knowledge in your chosen investment strategy. Choose one from the Skills in Part 5. Then go on courses, listen to podcasts, read all you can and then, when you have saved enough money, you will be good-to-go.

THE SCHOOL LEAVER'S GUIDE TO MONEY

THE SECOND RULE OF WEALTH:

PAY YOURSELF FIRST

Some people save, but dip into their savings for holidays or to buy clothes etc. You must think about savings differently.

Think of the money you pay into your savings account as the most important bill you have. Up there with council tax or rent. Try everything you can before you stop paying into your savings. Pay yourself first, this money is your future; never take money out of the account unless it is for an investment.

Call your savings account, 'My financial Freedom Account', and think of the money in there as someone else's, not for Christmas presents, holidays or treats. I know this sounds extreme, and it is, and you will need to be incredibly patient, but in the long-run it will be well worth it.

That way you know categorically that in the planned timescale, you will be on track to invest your money and become financially free.

Changing your mind-set

No matter what job you are in, even if you are on minimum wage, if you don't buy liabilities and buy assets you can become wealthy, it's just a matter of time.

For some people, it is extremely difficult to move from a consumer to a wealth mind-set, for two main reasons:

Peer pressure

Pressure to conform to your social group is a very strong force. It's a basic human need to want to be socially included and in some cases your personal development and financial progress could lead to people changing their attitude toward you. In the worst case, social exclusion. Most people find this very hard to deal with. I know this from experience, so again, be prepared for the naysayers and keep thinking of the long-term goal.

Self-discipline

Your friends may have nice cars and clothes and you will want these too; this is natural. But it's the quickest way to throw your money down the drain and remain poor. The problem is that we are fighting our ego, we see a flash car and associate that with a better-looking girlfriend or the approval of our mates. The media in collaboration with the corporations have been programming us to think this way for generations. Don't worry, you'll have all the flash cars you want, in time, paid for sustainably from your passive income. I will talk more on this in Skill 14.

I have reiterated a fair bit in this important section, because in truth, if you cannot make the transition to a wealth mind-set, there is little chance of you ever becoming wealthy. The good news is that if you do, it's not that difficult for the average person to achieve a good level of wealth in their lifetime. I know, I've done it and my sons are well on their way.

One caveat: the younger you start, the better your chances. If you are 16, you'll make it on any wage. But if you are 50, you'd better have some money to put in to buy a few houses or be earning a lot of money.

I'll leave you with a quote that drove me on to become financially free. This is by the late great Jim Rohn; please check him out:

*"If you don't find a way of earning money in
your sleep, you'll work till you die."*

If you want to know how to earn money in your sleep, read on.

PART 2:
WHAT IS MONEY?

....

Hopefully by now you have an understanding of what it is going to take to change your financial fortunes. I hope your head is in the right place and you are determined to make it happen.

Now let's get into some more background. In Part 2 I will explain what money is and is not, the types of money and where it comes from. You need to understand what money is and how it works in preparation for when you start investing, which I discuss in Parts 4 and 5. This grounding will help put the other skills into perspective.

By the end of Part 2 you will have a good understanding of:

4. Barter
5. Currency
6. Real Money – Gold and Silver
7. Fiat Currency
8. Where Does Money Come From
9. The Future of Money

SKILL 4: BARTER

In order to change the future, we have to understand the past.

A good understanding of the history of money and how it evolved to where we are today is an essential part of your investment toolkit.

Money in the form we know it today has only been around for a few hundred years. A system known as Barter was used for thousands of years before that.

Barter is when goods are exchanged in a trade. An example would be as follows:

Your wife asked you to go to market and bring home a pig. You have in your cart two chickens, which you are hoping to exchange for a pig.

You eventually find a person who has a pig and would like some eggs. She agrees to give you the pig in exchange for your two chickens and you are both happy.

But what if the pig owner feels her pig is worth four chickens, then there's no trade. But you don't want to upset the wife, so you explore two options.

You could choose the very messy option of chopping the porker in half and exchanging one half for two chickens. Or you could offer the pig owner something else to make up for the loss of two chickens, like the bag of grain you happen to have on your cart.

You can see how complicated barter could get and as civilisations grew the system couldn't cope.

Alongside barter, one of the early strategies used by pre-modern societies was to use credit to supplement the barter system.

In our example, this would be like the pig owner agreeing to take two chickens for the pig now, with a promise from the chicken owner to give the other two chickens sometime in the future.

In this case she would probably want something in addition to the two chickens to cover her inconvenience, maybe another chicken or a bag of grain. This was an early form of interest, interest on the loan of the half a pig.

As civilizations grew and became more complex the barter system became inadequate and people all over the world began to use more convenient forms of exchange, known as currency.

SKILL 5: CURRENCY

....

I'd heard the term currency over the years and assumed it meant money, but it does not. It is extremely important that you understand the difference between money and currency.

Currency is something you have in your pocket that everyone agrees has value. You can use that in exchange for chickens, for example.

Take a five-pound note or a pound coin: these are currency, not money. Currency has little to no value in itself.

For example, a five-pound-note is a worthless piece of paper, good for starting fires. What gives that paper its value is the government. They have decreed to the people that we must use the fiver to buy goods and that it is worth five pounds. When the people accept the government decree, the fiver has value.

If tomorrow the government said that fivers were useless, then they would revert to being worthless pieces of paper. If the government said that paper clips now had value and could be used to buy goods and services; assuming the people obeyed the government, then paperclips could suddenly be used to buy goods. Anything can be used as currency and throughout history the most unlikely things have.

History of Currency

Different forms of currency began to be adopted all over the world alongside and eventually replacing barter.

Let's use our chicken and pig analogy to explain how currency was a vast improvement on barter.

Let us assume that the currency the population is using are sea shells, as it has many times throughout history; and let's also assume that everyone in the land agrees that sea shells have a value, and that one chicken is worth five shells.

Therefore, I could buy two chickens anywhere in the land for ten shells. The shells would fit easily in my pocket and could be exchanged for any type of good or service. Very convenient.

The whole system would only work if the population agreed that shells had value. If you think about it, the only thing that gives the shells value, is the fact that the people believe they do; the shell, like the fiver, is worthless.

Having a currency that is lightweight and portable such as shells, notes or coins has several advantages over the barter system. It is much easier to carry than chickens, and it is divisible, unlike a pig.

Throughout history many things have been used as currency, including feathers, stones, grains, shells, animals and spices. But eventually all forms of post-modern currency broke down for one reason or another. For example, grains spoil over time, feathers damage easily, shells are different sizes and break easily.

The world needed a more reliable and stable currency that would stand the test of time, so eventually different types of 'coinage' began to be minted around the world which were much more robust and stood the test of time and eventually took over all other forms of currency.

The most important thing I want you to take from this section is:

Currency is not money, currency is just a medium of exchange that governments have decreed we, the people, use. But within itself it has no intrinsic value.

I remember when I was first introduced to this concept, I went around correcting everyone who referred to money and told them it was not money, it was currency. You tend to get a lot of blank looks, so in the end I gave up. Just know in your own mind that what you have known as money your entire life, is not money, as it has no value. It is just currency.

I shall refer to it as currency or money for the remainder of this book.

SKILL 6: REAL MONEY

....

Gold and silver

Two types of currency that do have intrinsic value are gold and silver, known as 'real money' in the investing world. But why are gold and silver real money? Because they have value in and of themselves and are a 'a store of value over time'. Let me explain.

A 1oz gold coin today could buy you the same value of goods it could a thousand years ago. This is why we say gold and silver are a store of value.

There is a well-known story that gold investors tell.

A thousand years ago a man could buy a toga, a pair of sandals and a good belt for 1oz of gold. That same 1oz of gold today, could buy you a good suit, shoes, shirt and belt today. Gold has kept its value and no other currency in history can claim this.

Why is this important?

If you had £1,500 pounds in the bank today in currency and you also had a 1oz gold coin in your drawer worth the same. In only one year from now your bank currency would have been eroded by inflation and be worth around 2%-3% less, and year-on-year its value will be eroded until it is worthless. But your gold coin will still buy you £1,500 worth of goods. It has kept its value and that is why people buy gold. Gold and silver are a store of value.

Coins

No one really knows when or where coins were first minted, but it is thought to be several thousand years ago. Countries all over the world began to adopt different types of coinage as currency.

Coins were minted from various metals and eventually became regularized in size and weight so they could be interchangeable.

The growth of empires and technology meant that different regions of the globe could trade and this eventually limited the number and types of coins in use and the metals they were minted from.

Ancient coins were minted in many different metals from copper, bronze and brass. Also, electrum, a mix of gold and silver, and gold and silver coins themselves.

Gradually, due to their exceptional qualities, only two metals stood the test of time and became universally accepted across the globe, those made from gold and silver; real money.

Definition of money

In his book, "Guide to Investing in Gold and Silver", Mike Maloney says that to count as "money", the item has to have the following qualities. Gold and silver are the only metals that meet all the criteria:

Money (gold and silver)

- Medium of exchange and unit of account
- Portable

- Durable
- Divisible
- Fungible (Interchangeable)
- A store of value

Currency (notes and coins in use)

- Medium of exchange and unit of account
- Portable
- Durable
- Divisible
- Fungible
- NOT a store of value.

The notes and coins we use meet most of the criteria for money, but they are not a store of value.

We will discuss investing in gold and silver in Skill 20, but for now, I hope this has made you realise that money as you knew it is not money, it is currency. Only gold and silver are real money and have been for thousands of years.

SKILL 7: FIAT CURRENCY

So far, we have discussed the barter system, currency, money and the significance of gold and silver. Now to focus on a certain type of currency, called Fiat Currency.

A 'fiat' is a decree, which is another name for an order. In this case by the government for the people to use notes and coins as currency. The only reason the notes in your pocket have value, is because the government has decreed it to be. As we know, currency has no intrinsic value.

Therefore, the money we currently use is called fiat currency, money with no intrinsic value.

From gold to fiat

Gold and silver coin have been used as money for thousands of years. But as society advanced and some people's wealth grew, gold and silver coins became too heavy and cumbersome to carry. People were also left wide open to theft. Eventually another more convenient system evolved.

It wasn't unusual for people with quantities of gold to deposit it with the gold lender for safe keeping. In return, the lender would issue a receipt to the depositor to be redeemed later for their gold.

As their vaults filled with other people's money, these shrewd gold lenders soon realised they could lend out some of the gold to other borrowers, at interest of course, and unbeknown to the previous depositor. This was the beginning of the banking system we know today, corrupt from the start.

As former president of the Bank of England Sir Josiah Stamp said, in his famous quotation,

"Banking was conceived in iniquity and was born in sin".

He was spot-on as we shall see in Skill 11.

This system, which became the beginnings of the banking system, was more convenient for depositors. Promissory notes were lighter to carry and safer than gold, and in time, exchanging notes became commonplace by the public.

The system eventually became known as 'The gold standard' currency (the receipts), backed and redeemable with gold.

The gold standard

The gold standard, currency backed by gold, was in force until 1971, when then president Richard Nixon took America off the gold standard and currency was no longer redeemable in gold. In other words, the government no longer backed currency with gold. From that moment, the world's currency became fiat, because of America's influence over the global monetary system. After 1971, gold lost its place as money and became a commodity metal, but to this day remains a store of value and the choice for many investors.

The problem with fiat currency

In a gold-backed system you could walk into a bank and ask for your currency to be exchanged for gold. This option does not exist today.

During the gold standard governments could only print the equivalent amount of currency to gold in their vaults. But now with the fiat system, governments are free to print as much currency as they see fit.

The problem for you and me is the more money in the economy the less our existing money is worth, its value is diluted. This is called inflation, which happens because there is more money chasing the same goods, causing prices to rise. For example, if a car dealer knows that three people have the money and want to buy his car, the price will go up.

The other issue with fiat currency is that it devalues just sitting in your bank due to inflation. A thousand in your bank today is worth less next year and less the following. If you think about it, this is just another form of taxation.

There is one very important thing to note about fiat currencies:

There have been thousands of fiat currencies throughout history and they all have one thing in common: they have all failed.

Ours will be no different. Our current system is on the cusp of failure and we will soon see a completely new financial system. At the time of writing there is a lot of speculation as to what this will be; some are saying a return to the gold standard, some say that the elites would never let this happen as their right to create money out of nothing and control the system will be taken away. I agree with that.

Some say the most likely system will be a fully digital currency where cash could even be made illegal. No one knows at this stage, but I will discuss the various contenders in Skill 9, The Future of Money.

Further information on this topic can be found in:

- The Guide to Investing in Gold and Silver, by Mike Maloney.
- The New Case for Gold, by Jim Rickards.
- Money, by Yuval Noah Harari.

SKILL 8:
WHERE DOES MONEY COME FROM?

How does the fiat currency we use get into society?

Ask a hundred people where money comes from and I doubt if even one will be right. You may be surprised to know that nearly all the currency we use today gets created out of thin air and gets into society in three ways:

- Notes and Coins – only 3% of money in existence.
- Central Bank Reserves – 18% of money in existence.
- Commercial Bank Money (Debt Money) – 79% of money in existence.

Notes and coins 3%

The only power in the land with authority to make the notes and coins in our pocket is the government. Any other person or entity caught printing or minting money would be sent to jail for forgery.

The Central Bank, in our case The Bank of England, is responsible for printing notes via nominated specialist printers, and the Royal Mint is responsible for minting coins. Both these types of currency are sometimes referred to as base money.

You may be very surprised to learn that all the coins and notes in the economy and in bank vaults, account for only 3% of the total currency in existence in the UK.

What, then, and where, is the other 97%?

Central bank reserves (bank deposits or demand deposits) 18%

This is one of those terms made difficult to understand on purpose. Central bank reserves mean, the money held in your bank account, sometimes also called demand deposits.

Due to the fractional reserve banking system, the bank is only obliged to keep a small fraction of your deposit and loan out the rest, as the money lenders of old did. Therefore, most of this currency is held in digital form.

It is used to transfer funds from one bank to another and can be converted to cash, 'on demand'.

Commercial bank money (debt money) 79%

I feel I should write this small but very significant paragraph in font 90 and in bold. It astonished me when I first heard this.

79% of our money is not created by our government, but out of thin air by banks, when they lend money. Currency is created when a bank lends money.

Since most of the currency held in our accounts is in digital form, many feel that commercial banks are responsible for the full 97% of the total money in existence.

By the way, someone pays interest on every penny of that money, created from nothing.

We will explore this further and the not-so-good implication to you, in Skill 11, The Monetary System.

SKILL 9: THE FUTURE OF MONEY

At the time of writing, the global monetary system is in chaos. Many experts believe it is collapsing, with the globalist central bankers propping-up and extending the current system by pumping in trillions of dollars, while desperately trying to develop the new system.

No one knows what that will be, but many believe it will be a new 'digital system of exchange', and currency as we know it will no longer exist.

This is a rapidly moving situation and many institutions, including the international monetary fund, IMF, world bank, central banks all over the world, commercial banks, the crypto community and even large corporations such as Facebook and Google are vying for position, putting forward alternative currency systems.

We are in uncharted waters, so it makes sense to get educated and understand what the possibilities could be when our existing system eventually collapses. One tip: keep away from the mainstream, or as we call it, lamestream financial media, they are always late to the party and the advice they give is not in your interests but in the interests of the unseen masters they serve. All media outlets globally are owned by only six corporations, and this explains why the narrative is always the same across all lamestream media.

Do keep informed though, but through the alternative media such as Brandnewtube, Rumble, Bitchute and Podcasts. I did not refer you to YouTube, as they have been censoring content and taking down thousands of channels lately. The ones they feel do not agree with the lamestream narrative. That is not freedom of speech.

These are some experts I'd recommend you follow. These folks actually run very successful financial businesses, rather than just commentating on events.

- Simon Dixon – Bitcoin and general finance.
- Mike Mahoney – Gold and general finance advice.
- Peter Schiff – Gold and general financial.
- Robert Kiyosaki – General financial.
- James Rickards – General financial.

Quantum computers

I need to introduce you to the game changing 'Quantum Computers', as this technology could redefine our financial system and everything else in our world.

These machines are seriously fast. Google announced it has a quantum computer that is 100 million times faster than any classical computer in its lab.

> *"Every day, we produce 2.5 Exabytes of data. That number is equivalent to the content on 5 million laptops."*

How close are we to a commercial quantum computer? In 2019, IBM showcased its first commercial quantum computer. In January 2020, the company claimed at the Consumer Electronics Show, that:

> *"We are now in the decade of quantum computing".*

The implication of quantum computers has made a global currency very achievable. So be on the lookout for a new digital currency and the gradual phasing out of cash, being helped along conveniently by the Covid pandemic.

Bitcoin

Will Bitcoin survive quantum computing?

Because they are extremely powerful, quantum computers may eventually be able to break many encryption schemes that are currently in widespread use. Cryptocurrency is at risk because Bitcoin and other cryptocurrencies rely on encryption for their security.

It is said that a calculation that could not be done by any computer currently on Earth, could be done in less than a second on a quantum computer.

> "If quantum computing is a spear, Public Key Encryption is like a shield made of tissue paper."
> **Craig Costello, Cryptographer, Ted Talk.**

Also, government intervention could be a major issue for Bitcoin and other cryptocurrencies. Governments have proven in the past that they can outlaw gold, for example, so I see no reason why this couldn't happen to cryptocurrencies if they interfered with the elite's global financial agenda.

For these reasons, I'd not invest in crypto personally, but I am no expert, I have only a basic knowledge. Please refer to Simon Dixon and his book, 'Bank to the Future', before you rule out cryptocurrency. I'm sure Simon will have a different view.

Paper and coin

You don't have to be an expert to understand that the government does not want paper currency. The Covid-19 Pandemic was a great opportunity for governments to spread the word that you could be infected by using paper notes. Whether this is the case or not, we shall never know, but many shops will not accept cash these days, however unlawful this may be, and governments are positively encouraging this action.

Many alternative media journalists feel this is all part of a long-term plan by the globalists to have 'financial reset'. Many believe this could be the biggest transfer of wealth away from the masses and towards the elite class, in history. Cash could be removed and replaced with a new globally-centralised financial exchange system, and many experts feel this could be the case in the not-so-distant future.

New global financial system?

Many central banks are as we speak developing digital currencies. Many people believe that the new system will not even be based on currency, but on a completely new digital transaction system, based on a digital wallet which is downloaded and would replace your bank account. Government welfare payments and wages could be deposited into the wallet, which would manage all your transactions.

You cannot think of a digital currency in terms of, say, a credit card. They are very different. A digital currency is a piece of computer code, which can be programmed to do anything. All your transactions could be fully traceable instantly by governments and large corporations. They will know where you spend your money and what on, and tax could be taken at source.

We could be moving to an economy where our freedoms and privacy just do not look the same as they used to. Any radical reform of the monetary system could remove your personal freedoms and privacies. "We'll give you money, but you do what we say."

Because the new digital currency is computer code, governments could programme the code to expire. For example, many believe that as Covid displaces so many jobs and small businesses, we are heading toward a Universal Basic Income, UBI, which could replace all welfare schemes. This could provide the population with a minimum level of financial security, but would definitely come with strings.

For example, if the government wants you to spend more money to get the economy moving and keep inflation steady, it can put an expiry date on your currency. If you do not spend the money by a particular date, it could actually disappear. They could even dictate where you spend your money. If they wanted to promote one corporation over another, say a global corporate such as Amazon over small local businesses, your currency could be coded only to be spent with Amazon.

We are in the middle of one of the most radical reforms of the financial systems in history. When we come out of the other side, the monetary system could have more of an impact on our personal freedoms than we have ever seen in history.

Many believe that the global health crisis we are experiencing was designed to prepare the people for radical change. For example, the 'digital health passport' being pushed by governments of the world in a coordinated effort which is unprecedented. To what end is yet to be seen.

On the other hand, Bitcoin and other blockchain currencies could exist outside of the mainstream financial system, giving people a great alternative and complete autonomy to the user. What is unknown at this stage is the adoption levels – as of today it is virtually impossible to buy your groceries with Bitcoin, so we have no choice but to opt in to mainstream banking.

The future may make you choose between a blockchain-based monetary system where you own your own money outside the financial system and have the privacy that comes with that. Or a central bank or large corporate digital currency, where doing so gives organisations and governments access to all your privacy, and forces you to give up many of your freedoms.

The choice could depend to a certain extent on convenience. If the various cryptocurrencies are more widely adopted, it could be possible in future to stay completely outside of the fiat currency system. The wise investor would probably use the fiat system for day-to-day purchases such as food and essential items, but hold the majority of their wealth outside of the mainstream, where the risks of losing your wealth would be less.

My advice here would be before your currency devalues sitting in the bank, invest what money you do have in the bank now on appreciating assets such as gold or property.

PART 3: BANKS

Josiah Charles Stamp, former director of the Bank of England, said:

"Banking was conceived in iniquity and was born in sin. The bankers own the earth. Take it away from them, but leave them the power to create money, and with the flick of the pen they will create enough deposits to buy it back again. But, if you wish to remain the slaves of bankers and pay the cost of your own slavery, let them continue to create money and control credit."

Mayer Anselm Rothschild said:

"Permit me to issue and control the money of a nation, and I care not who makes its laws."

One of, if not the main purposes of my writing this book was to give you knowledge of the banking system and how it has been screwing the public for centuries, but never more than it is today.

Banks

Whoever gives any thought to banks? They, like the BBC, are just trusted institutions that have always been there.

But there is a dark side to banks – and the BBC for that matter, but that's for another book. They are rarely if ever mentioned in the lamestream news; the bankers like to keep it that way, out of the public eye and away from scrutiny.

Banks have a massive effect on all areas of our lives and you'd certainly take more notice if you knew what they get up to.

Banking language is purposely shrouded in jargon, which only those very close to the industry can understand, keeping the public in blissful ignorance.

Those who own the banks run every aspect of the world and it's no wonder: they create 97% of the world's money and lend it to whom they choose. They touch every area of our lives every day and not in a good way. But don't just take my word for it.

Mike Malone is a world renowned financial expert; in his book Guide to Investing in Gold and Silver, he discusses that:

The banking system has been designed to take money from the masses and direct that money to the elites who own the banking system. They have been robbing the people for generations.

For these reasons, a sound knowledge of the banking system and what they get up-to, is essential.

Banking has become very complex, not even understood by most who work in the industry. Those who own banks do not want you to understand how the system works. The system has kept the elites at the top of the financial food-chain for hundreds of years.

Banks and those who own them have been and still are responsible for many of the world's atrocities throughout history, wars and evils of the world and my aim here is to give you insight so that you may free yourself from the grasp of bankers.

I hope by the time you get to the end of Skill II, you will have an understanding of the banking system and that will provoke you to research further.

A great place to start is 'The Creature from Jekyll Island' by G. Edward Griffin, which sets out the story of how Central Banking began and the fraud they have been committing under our noses ever since. Anyone serious about protecting their future must read this eye-opening book.

By the end of Part 3 you will have a good understanding of the different types of bank and how the modern banking system works. But most of all, you will start to realise how the 'real' world works.

10. Types of Banks
11. How the Banking System Works

SKILL 10: TYPES OF BANK

To lighten things up a little before we get heavy again in Skill 11, let me first introduce you to the types of bank there are out there and what they do.

Universal bank

Universal in that they provide all the usual products and services that banks provide under one roof, but are usually split into separate divisions, such as:

- Retail Banking – providing services to the public.
- Commercial Banking – providing services to businesses.
- Investment Banking – providing services to investors and investment institutions.

The big four as they are known in the UK – Barclays, HSBC, Lloyds Banking Group and The Royal Bank of Scotland Group – are all universal banks with different divisions.

Commercial banking

The division of universal banks that deals with companies, usually small to medium enterprises, SMEs, are known as commercial banks. In the US, these are called retail banks.

Retail bank (UK)

This is the public face of banking with branches that deal directly with the public.

In some banks, such as Barclays, the high street branch is combined to provide services to the public and business. Therefore, when you walk into a branch, you are walking into a commercial and a retail bank. From now on I will use the term 'commercial bank' to describe both.

Investment banks

The big four banks each have investment arms. Investment banks are the sell side of the city, creating financial products to sell to big companies and big financial institutions. Investment banks were a big part of the cause of the 2008 financial crash.

Following the financial crisis of 2008 and the tax-payer bail-outs, government regulation forced banks to separate their investment side into legal entities in order to protect the public from the speculative investments of some of these banks.

Private banks

Some banks offer more personal services to high-net-worth individuals and businesses, particularly family businesses, who may be interested in transferring wealth down the generations and tend to have more complex financial situations than the general public.

Private banks offer a wide range of services such as traditional banking, investing, estate and succession planning.

Some of these banks have been serving their customers for generations and are known for fiercely protecting the interests of their customers.

Central banks

If you do a Google search you will get the official narrative as to what a Central bank does. This is different from the role they actually carry out as we shall see in Skill 11. But nevertheless, this is the official narrative:

Central banks are banks to the commercial banks and the government.

In the UK, the central bank is the Bank of England, BOE. In the USA the Federal Reserve, known as the FED, and for Europe it is the European Central Bank, ECB.

The main role of a central bank is to manage the country's money supply. The roles of a central bank are as follows:

- Manage the nation's money supply. Through activities such as setting interest rates, setting bank reserve requirements, which is the amount of money that commercial banks must hold in reserve at the central bank.
- Stabilizing the money and capital markets. In other words, provide short term liquidity (money) to support any shortfalls in banks.
- Serving as a lender of last resort for financial institutions in need of reserves during insolvency or financial crisis. I.e. when a commercial bank cannot meet its financial obligations it provides liquidity to prevent the banking system from failing.
- Provides price stability by controlling inflation through controlling the money supply.
- Prints bank notes in circulation.

In most countries, central banks are independent private companies, profit making organisations, responsible to shareholders separate from their government, like the FED for example.

The BOE was nationalised in 1946 and became an 'independent public organisation' in 1998, owned by the government, and is supposed to be independent in its setting of monetary policy.

In reality, there is a complex mix of ownership with central banks around the world, which varies from fully privately owned, to a mix of private/public, to fully public. The true ownership of most central banks is kept from public record, shrouded in secrecy.

On-line banks

There are numerous on-line banks. Nearly all big banks offer an on-line only facility linked to all accounts. But there are a growing number of banks which are exclusively on-line with no physical outlets; which means some of these banks can be very competitive with their fees, some even offering higher interest rates.

On-line banking is very convenient. Anything can be done on-line such as transfers, payment, shopping etc. Accounts can be accessed day or night and information is instantaneous, which can be very useful when you need to pay for something on the spot. All this makes on-line banking very attractive.

There is only one down-side to on-line-only banking, and that is some people feel that there could be a security risk from hackers. Also, there is the question as to what would happen should the internet go down. For these reasons I'd not personally go fully on-line and prefer the comfort of an established high-street bank.

SKILL II: THE MONETARY SYSTEM

....

A study of the monetary system is really a study of the banking system, because it is the banks who run the world's money supply. Surprisingly, governments are the same as you and me, in that we both are little more than borrowers to the banks, as we shall see.

Like many before, the worldwide monetary system is failing and many experts think it will collapse soon.

Perhaps one of the greatest challenges of our age is to discover what will replace the current system.

It is very important for you as an investor to understand how the world's money system works. Knowing the current system will enable you to better understand whatever system comes next.

I am going to share with you an extract from Mike Maloney's Hidden Secrets of Money series, which can be found on YouTube. Mike explains this complicated subject better than I. But first an explanation of some of the terms Mike uses.

Bonds

Bonds are no more than government IOUs. Governments issue bonds when they need cash. Bonds are for different periods of time with different interest rates. For example, a £1m bond of 10-year term at a 5% interest. This means a bondholder pays £1m to the government for the bond and the government pays an annual interest to the bondholder (the coupon) of 5% annually. At the end of the term the government pays back the original £1m.

Bank deposits

A bank deposit is money you put into the bank. When you deposit money into the bank, the bank is not holding the deposit to be safely held on trust for you. Instead you are loaning your currency to the bank to do with as they will, within certain legal limits.

Fractional reserve lending.

The bank only needs to keep a fraction of the money you deposit. They are allowed to loan the rest out at interest. The fractional-reserve rate is usually set at 10%. But this fluctuates, and at this present time it is zero.

That means the bank can now loan out 90% of your deposit. The bank must hold 10% just in case you want some of it back; this is called vault cash.

But even though the bank has lent 90 of your 100, your account still says you have 100. How? Because the bank created another 90 of digital currency out of thin air when they loaned out 90% of your deposit.

This means that where there was 100 in existence there is now 190. The bank, by giving a loan, has created new currency.

The borrower of your deposit then takes your 90% and buys something. The seller deposits your 90% into their account and the process repeats. Someone can borrow 90% of that.

An initial deposit of 100 can create up to 1000 of bank credit.

This expands the currency supply by 92-96%.

The problem with this is that the additional currency causes prices to rise as there is more money in existence. This is the definition of inflation, the expansion of the currency supply.

How the financial system works

- It all starts when governments need money.
- To raise money the government instructs the Treasury to issue a bond.
- The Treasury then holds a 'bond auction' and big banks bid to buy the bond. The winning bank buys the bond from the government. The government gets money, the bank has a bond.
- The bank takes the bond over to the Bank of England, BOE, to sell the bond for money. The BOE creates currency out of thin air and buys the bond from the bank.
- The BOE now has bonds building up and the Treasury has money.
- This process repeats over and over, enriching the banks.
- The interest owed to the BOE on the bonds is our national debt and the unwitting public picks up the bill through taxes.
- The Treasury then deposits the currency into the various departments of the government.
- Government spends money on government contracts, war, social programmes.
- Those working on these contracts deposit their pay into the banks. Our labour is what gives the currency value.
- Fractional reserve banking is then applied to our deposited money, and the banks expand the money supply by 92-96%, reducing the value of the pound in your pocket.
- We work hard to pay the Inland Revenue taxes, who give our tax money to the Treasury, to pay back the interest owed on the bond to the BOE, who printed the money out of thin air.
- The cycle repeats and our national debt increases.

The whole thing is one big scam.

Thank you to Mike Malone, The Hidden Secrets of Money Series. I recommend watching the ten-part series on YouTube.

Much of our taxes are not used to pay for schools, hospitals, roads etc, they are used to pay the principal and interest on the bonds that the BOE bought from the banks.

Before the establishment of the BOE, there was no income tax at all. The tax we pay is syphoned off to the owners of the system, the silent owners. Our whole system is based on borrowing and debt.

The system is evil. It funnels wealth from the working population to the shareholders of the BOE, the government and the banking sector. It causes great disparity of wealth between the rich and the working class.

This system relies on the public being ignorant of its working.

This summary gives you the highlights, but hopefully it will provoke you to research this fraudulent system further.

Some good sources of information are:

- The Creature from Jekyll Island by G. Edward Griffin.
- Mike Maloney and his YouTube series Hidden Secrets of Money.
- Guide to Investing in Gold and Silver by Mike Maloney.
- James Corbett of the Corbett Report which can be found at corbettreport.com/federal reserve

Reference to lamestream research such as Wikipedia, Google or any lamestream reference, will almost definitely not bring up a true representation, as they are wholly controlled by the very people who have set-up the banking system. Who also, incidentally, control the lamestream.

The history of banking

The history of banking is a scandalous one. The government actually gave away its right to print and control the country's money supply way back in the seventeenth century. King William the third of England needed money to rebuild his war ships following a devastating defeat in the nine-years' war.

A Scottish banker named William Patterson came up with a solution to form a privately-owned organisation to loan the government £1.2 million pounds at 8% interest. The BOE was formed, a completely privately-owned business with the government charter to print money out of thin air and lend it to the government, at interest of course.

The name BOE was a carefully chosen and deceptive name, to give the public the impression this was a government-owned organisation, when in fact it was a privately-owned profit-making company.

Unlike the FED, the BOE became publicly owned as late as 1998, but its true ownership is still shrouded in mystery.

Who owns your money?

There is a big misconception about commercial banks. Most people think that when you deposit money in the bank it is safely sitting there ready for you to draw out whenever you want. This is not the case. When you deposit money in a bank, you are lending it to the bank to do with as they please; you become a creditor of the bank. In other words, the bank owes you the money, but your money becomes the legal property of the bank.

How do banks create our currency?

Another misconception, is that when you take out a loan, you are borrowing some other depositor's money with the bank acting as an intermediary, but this is not the case. The money you receive when you take out a loan is not some other depositor's money but brand-new money created by the bank. Banks are the creators of our money and every pound created, is created in debt and owed interest on.

When you take out a bank loan, the money you receive is brand new money brought into existence by typing it to your account. Bank money is created when they give out loans and all that money is created in debt and interest is owed on every penny.

Let's say you need a car loan or a mortgage and your bank agrees to lend you the money. Numbers are typed into your account and like magic new currency is created out of thin air. The money supply of the country has just increased by you taking out the loan. That new money was created as debt, and this has a big implication.

Interest is owed on every pound of lending. The more debt a bank has the more interest they receive. Bankers love to lend money, they are incentivised to lend money. Why? Because the more money they lend, the more interest they receive. More interest means bigger bonuses and more profit for the shareholders.

As the creators and lenders of the money supply, banks have such a huge impact on the global economy. This is why governments go to great lengths to protect banks and even bail them out with taxpayer money if they get into trouble, like they did in 2008. If a big bank were to fail the global money supply would be reduced overnight. Businesses are so dependent on banking institutions that if they were allowed to fail, the entire economy could collapse with it. For this reason, central banks refuse to allow these banking institutions to fail.

To be clear, banks create money out of thin air, lend it to you and you pay them interest on that debt. Nice work if you can get it. But there are big implications for you and me.

How bank money affects the economy

The fact that government allows banks to create money is very bad for the people and especially small businesses. It means that we have a bunch of bankers who must earn profit for their shareholders, deciding 'who' gets the money in the economy, not the democratically elected government.

Banks lend to the entities that best suit the bank, not the people. Bankers are truly running the world.

Here's that quote again from Rothschild:

> *"Permit me to issue and control the money of a nation, and I care not who makes its laws".*

He should know, the Rothschilds are among the few families who do control much of the banking system and the world.

If you think the governments run the world, think again. The banks run the world and they are designed, controlled and owned by families like the Rothschilds' banking dynasty and the Rockefellers, for their benefit, not yours.

Who do banks lend to?

As you would expect from a private company, banks lend money based on what they feel represent their best interests, not the people's. They lend to certain sectors and exclude others to the detriment of small businesses and the country.

The general split of total bank lending in the UK can be seen from the figures below:

- Loans to Housing   40%
- Loans to the speculative financial sector   37%
- Loans to small businesses   13%
- Personal loans and credit cards   10%

Loans to housing

40% of all bank lending goes into the housing sector. This may seem like a good idea, but is in fact a major problem.

The more money made available by banks for housing investment, the more property prices will rise because more money is chasing the same house.

This happened in 2008 when house prices became so unaffordable, that people started defaulting on their loans. The problem is that governments have little control over the banking system, and the banks are making the same mistakes today. The result: a whole generation of people who cannot afford to get on the property ladder.

When I bought my first house in 1984, it was relatively easy to afford a nice three-bed on my carpenter's wage. Most working people back then could afford a mortgage; my friends and I didn't give it much thought. You just bought a house when you were ready.

A young carpenter today cannot afford the same house I bought. Pro rata property prices are much higher. This is the result of banks pumping loans into housing and central banks keeping interest rates low.

Banks make their decision regarding who to lend to, based on who they feel will be most likely to pay them back and who they can charge the most interest, not on who needs the money most.

The banks' perception is that home owners are less risky than businesses, as home owners will fight to keep a roof over their family's heads. The perception is that businesses, on the other hand, have a high chance of defaulting on their loans, so banks do not like lending to them. This has a detrimental effect on our high-streets and small businesses in general.

I know this first hand. I have noticed in our business that it is more difficult to get bank lending. Even with our 36-year history with Barclays, strong reserves and property assets. For most small businesses, borrowing is all but impossible.

This lending policy has pushed property prices up and made small businesses suffer, which has led to unemployment. Until this system changes, nothing will change.

Loans to the finance sector

Money making more money – 37% of total lending goes to the financial sector for speculative investment. This can make banks a lot of money, but creates no value at all for the economy. It provides few jobs for working people. Like the housing sector, this is simply money producing more money, making the rich richer.

Loans to small businesses

The very core of capitalism is credit. Without credit, entrepreneurial dreams cannot become reality. With only 13% of bank money available to SMEs, no wonder they are going under by the thousands in the UK and globally, helped massively by the recent pandemic.

Small businesses have always been the backbone of any country and by far the biggest employer. They create entrepreneurs who fire our economy and create future employment.

The truth is the highstreets are dying, manufacturing is virtually non-existent, private infrastructure projects are rare... the list goes on. In short, the lending policies of banks are creating unemployment and decimating the country.

The opposite is true for the multi-nationals. Amazon, Google, Facebook and Big Pharma are getting richer and richer and creating monopolies.

Where will it end?

Personal loans and credit cards

You also have the power to create money. When you pay for goods on your credit card you are creating new money.

The boom and bust cycle

We've all heard of a bubble, but what is it and how does it happen?

A bubble occurs when there is a very high inflation in the price of a specific good or service over a short period of time.

As previously explained, if banks put the majority of lending into housing then house prices will rise, because more money is chasing the available housing stock. This process will continue until eventually prices become so high that the average person cannot afford the repayments on their mortgage or rent.

At this point the bubble bursts. People start defaulting on their rents and landlords on their loans and banks start to suffer. If this continues it can lead to bank failures like it did in 2008. This is the inevitable conclusion of a system where banks are allowed to create money and lend to whom they like.

However, the government will never let big banks fail, as it will be too destructive to the economy, so the course of action so far has been to bail out the banks using taxpayer money, re-capitalising banks and it's back to business as usual. Instead of addressing the structural problems with the banking system, the government has taken the short-term option and kicked the can down the road for someone else to deal with.

Bailout

As described above a bailout refers to the government using taxpayer money to save the banks from going under, known as 'recapitalising' the bank.

This happened in 2008 and the public were not happy. Should banks require assistance again, it is doubtful that they would use taxpayer bailouts in the first instance for fear of public retribution; rather they may resort to bail-ins, which the governments could view as more acceptable to at least most of the public.

Bail-in

You will be horrified to know that banks have the right to take your money if they are in trouble. This happened recently in Cyprus, where deposits greater than 100,000 euros were seized to cover Cypriot bank debts.

As discussed, this is a real threat even in the UK and could affect small businesses and the public with more than £85,000 in their account.

In the UK, we have a deposit insurer scheme known as the Financial Services Compensation Scheme (FSCS). It covers up to £85,000 per depositor per bank. But it is widely thought that should banks begin to fail there would be insufficient funds to indemnify all depositors.

If you are a person who has more than £85,000 in any one bank, you would do well to open another account to spread your risk. But do not tell the bank the reason you are opening the account; they are only interested in you if they think you are going to borrow money, so they can charge you interest.

PART 4:
WEALTH KNOWLEDGE

....

We can now put the unsavoury background information behind us and move on to some topics that will really benefit you in your investing career.

Knowledge of these financial concepts is essential to your investing career. They are generic to any type of investing and will help you identify a good or a bad deal.

By the end of Part 4 you will have a good understanding of the following:

12. Assets & Liabilities
13. Good and Bad Debt
14. Passive Income
15. Capital Growth
16. Compounding
17. What Is Leverage?

SKILL 12: ASSETS & LIABILITIES

When I hear the terms assets and liabilities, my mind always goes back to my old mentor, John Trueman. John was the only person who told me repeatedly not to buy cars. Did I listen? No, but I wish I had, I could have been financially free 20 years earlier.

John taught me this:

The key to your future prosperity depends entirely on whether you buy assets that go up in value (appreciating assets) or liabilities that go down in value (depreciating assets).

If you did that alone, you would probably be wealthy by the time you were 35 if you started at 18.

But let's be clear as to what assets are.

It's not good enough to say an asset is something you own. Because many things you own cost money and go down in value, like a car, for example. But then a collector's car that appreciates could be an asset. You have to be careful and think about everything you buy.

I want you to start thinking like an investor. From now on, this is the test you should apply for assets and liabilities.

Assets must be something:

- You own that maintains or goes up in value.
- You own that gives you a return.
- You may not own that gives you a return.

Liability is something:

- That costs you money.
- That goes down in value.

You need to be clear that if it costs you money at all on an ongoing basis, it is not an asset. It is a liability.

Let's go through a list of common things to see whether they are assets or liabilities to familiarise you with the concept:

Your car

Unless it appreciates in value – and it will almost certainly not – then it doesn't meet any of the tests for an asset. It's a liability, perhaps your biggest.

In my case I could have been financially free at a very young age had it not been for the hundreds of thousands I've wasted on cars. Silly boy.

Your home

An asset, right? Wrong, in most cases. It may well go up in value over time (appreciate) although this is not certain, but you pay a mortgage, council tax, utility bills and upkeep. It's a liability. A necessary one, agreed, but a liability.

By the way, some investors I know would never own a home. They rent as it's more tax efficient and the landlord pays for upkeep. They use the money they save to buy more assets which provide them a return and that return pays their rent.

A rental property you own

If the process is managed correctly most certainly yes, this is a great asset. Your rent covers the mortgage and gives you a monthly income, and in most cases the property will go up in value over time. Win-win and a great legacy.

I will go into property investing in much more detail in Skill 19 and provide a step-by-step investment plan.

A bicycle

Does not meet any of the asset tests, it's a liability. But you could argue that it keeps you fit and enables you to keep healthy and reduces stress. You could also use it to get to work and save petrol while keeping fit at the same time. So, I'll let you have that one as an asset. But not if you have three bicycles.

Gold or silver

As discussed in Skill 6. Gold and silver are a store of value over time.

Remember the story about the man buying a toga, sandals and belt for 1oz of gold. And that the same one ounce of gold buying a man's suit, shirt, shoes and belt today. It has kept its value over the years.

It meets the first test, in that it maintains its value and at certain times increases in value. It does not, however, give you a return on your money, so investors tend to buy it if they have cash sitting around doing nothing, or as a hedge against uncertainties in the economy; safe in the knowledge that gold and silver have kept their value for thousands of years.

Some prominent investors believe that gold should represent no more than ten percent of one's portfolio. We have much less as we like our money to give us a return.

Buy needs not wants

We all need to live so you'll have to buy some liabilities like food and the other essentials of life. Where possible, only buy good organic food as this will help to keep you healthy and prolong life. It's definitely worth spending more money on good food; anything else is a false economy.

Only you can know what you really 'need' in your life to be content as opposed to what you 'want'. The more you live by the philosophy of buying needs and not wants, the quicker you will become wealthy. But this has to be tempered with common sense. It's no good giving up your social life and getting depressed. Try to live as normal a life as possible, but at the same time minimise the wants and the liabilities.

I think that you can begin to see that over a lifetime of buying appreciating assets as opposed to depreciating liabilities, the difference to your wealth will be staggering, as we have seen in Skill 3.

Unfortunately, most of the population are influenced by media advertising or peer pressure to buy stuff they do not really need; people are obsessed with buying worthless stuff. A wealthy person buys on a needs-only basis, limiting the wants. Until such time that the passive income is enough to pay for the wants-a-plenty.

Over a lifetime, your accumulated spending patterns can either make you rich or poor.

SKILL 13: GOOD AND BAD DEBT

Learn to Love Good Debt and Hate Bad Debt

What is good and what is bad? The average person thinks all debt is bad. My dad takes much pride in telling me he is debt-free. "No mortgage, son, no loans, nothing." This is all well and good, but it won't make you rich.

I want you to start thinking that a certain type of debt can be very good indeed for your financial health. Good debt is the type that earns you money. Take on as much good debt as you can.

Good debt

I first started buying houses to rent out in my late thirties. Although it was a very good thing to do, I didn't understand why it was so good and how it could have changed my life back then, had I not sold all the properties. Back then I just bought the houses because the firm had spare money and houses were cheap at the time.

I bought seven houses in quick succession in Southend-on-Sea. The average price was £68,000 and I bought all of them with a 75% loan to value buy-to-let interest only mortgage.

We cover this type of mortgage in detail in Skill 28, but for now it's good enough to know that we had to put in 25% cash deposit, that's £17,000 for each house and the bank lent us the other 75%.

The mortgage repayments were around £200 per month and the rental income was around £550. That's a clear £350 profit every month, forever.

This is good debt, when the debt makes you money.

I think you can understand that you want as much safe good debt as you can get. I say safe because there is one caveat.

A good investor always keeps a healthy margin of error in their portfolio. For example, say the interest rates were to shoot up to 5% or house prices were to drop by 20%, would you still make money or lose everything like so many in 2008? A good investor builds in a healthy margin of error and pays down debt as soon as possible to reduce the loan amount to safe territory. We try to keep our entire portfolio under 60% loan to value and we are aiming at 50%. Even in the worst of crashes 50% LTV should be safe.

Good debt can make you rich, but safe good debt can make you rich and sleep at night.

Ray Spooner

Bad debt

Bad debt has the opposite effect.

I mentioned earlier that before I became aware of the wealth mindset I bought a lot of cars, and for most of us, cars will be a big liability and the worst example of bad debt.

One particular flash car I bought was a Porsche. I really wanted one, I saw it as a sign of status to what I'd achieved in life. I liked the thought of showing off this beautiful vehicle to my business colleagues, family and friends. I was full of ego at that age.

My salesperson friend told me that he can tell when someone is going to buy a car the first time they look at it. He said if their eyes are fixed on the car to the point where they are almost licking their lips whilst making noises like, wow and corr. He knew he had a sucker sale as he called it.

This was me, I'm afraid. It's no exaggeration to say that buying cars instead of houses caused me to have to work another 20 years of my life. Although in reality I'd never stop working anyway. I should say, spending my time as I please 20 years earlier.

So why is getting into debt to buy a car or any other liability so bad for your wealth?

From memory, the Porsche was about £49,000. I had to come up with 15% deposit. So that was £8,400 cash. The repayments over four years were around £950 per month based on a deal where I could return the car at the end of the term. (Detailed in Skill 26.)

So, in four years that car cost me £54,000. Down the drain never to be seen again; and to be honest, after a few weeks of having the car the novelty wore off anyway and it was an uncomfortable drive.

To put that into context.

I'd put £17,000 each deposit on the houses I'd bought in Southend and they were earning me £350 per month.

The car over four years cost me £54,000. That's enough for three deposits.

The three houses would all return me £350 each, that's £1050 per month rent.

So rather than earning £1050 per month forever, I was paying £950 per month.

To make matters worse, if I'd have bought the three houses first, the rent would have paid for the monthly payments on the car, and this is exactly what the rich do. They let their 'cash flow' pay for their toys. Amazing, isn't it.

This brings us to Rule three:

RULE 3:

USE PASSIVE INCOME TO BUY LIABILITIES.

SKILL 14: PASSIVE INCOME

Passive income is a wonderful thing, it's the end game. It's what every investor strives for and what every wealthy person has. Passive income is making money while you sleep or you're in the Bahamas on the beach. Sounds good, doesn't it? You can have it too, so read on.

Passive income is the income you derive from your investment. In the example in the previous Skill, the rent would be the passive income, commonly known as 'cash flow'. If you bought shares, the passive income would be the dividend.

Passive income will enable you and your family to live a life free from money worries and it will give you the freedom to do what you want when you want with whom you want. What better way to go through life could there be?

All the hard work required to get passive income is done up-front; and it is hard work. In the case of a rental property there is a lot of work, time and cash required in the front end, for passive income to drop out at the back end.

Please do not underestimate these words, they are easy to say, but when you are working hours to get your property refurbished, viewing tens of properties miles away or arguing with builders, it can all seem too much at times.

Finding, buying, refurbishing and letting a house will take over six months, but be patient; when complete, the passive income drops into your bank forever. It's an amazing deal in the long-run.

But there is one thing you must understand about passive income:

No income is truly passive.

Using rental property as the example. If you rely on the rental income to live on, you'd better make sure that property is going to be a good cash-cow for the rest of your life. Several things could go wrong: a tenant not paying rent, roof leaks, tenants leaving, emergencies such as burst pipes all need to be attended to. If you happen to be in the Bahamas at the time this could be a real problem and you'll soon see how passive your income is not.

But if you had the foresight to employ a letting agent to deal with such problems while you are away, then it could be more passive.

You can understand the degree to which your investment is passive depends on the amount of time and effort you have put into setting up your investment in the first place.

But even with all the planning and foresight in the world, no investment is ever truly passive; it will need some degree of management or input from you, and rightly so, it is very important to protect your investment and no one will do that better than you.

SKILL 15: CAPITAL GROWTH

When I bought the properties in Southend I paid £68,000 on average each. Three years later they sold for £94,000. I made £26,000 x 7 properties. That's a profit of £182,000 in just over three years.

At that time, just before 2007, properties were sky rocketing. But had I sold after the crash in 2008 I'd have probably lost money. Therefore, a certain amount of investment education is required to know when to buy and sell, which I will cover in detail in Skill 19.

The £182,000 is what's known as the 'capital appreciation', the amount they went up in value.

This is the ultimate aim of any investor. Not only did I enjoy three years of rental income, sometimes called passive income, cash flow or yield, but the properties had appreciated in value a whacking £182,000. Shame I sold them when I did.

Strategy

When investors consider an investment, they view it from two perspectives:

- Yield or Cash Flow
- Capital Growth

The yield is the cash flow generated from the investment. In terms of property, the rent you receive after costs is known as the net return or net cash flow, the amount left after taking away all costs.

Different things are important to different people – some value cash flow and some capital appreciation. Some both, like me.

Before you invest you should assess your investment from these two perspectives.

For example, if I were to buy an averagely priced property in the North of England, generally speaking it would be a lot cheaper than a property in the South. But the rental income would not be much different. The investor could pay much less for the Northern property and still get a similar rent. This is good and may incentivise a Southern investor to make the journey up the M1 to their investment area, discussed in Skill 19.

But you have to consider that in general, a Northern property will not go up in value as quickly as a property in the South. Therefore, the capital appreciation will be much less.

Whether you buy in the North for cash flow or the South for growth is dependent on your personal circumstances and where you live. What is important is having the investment skillset to understand the pros and cons of different types of investment, and we shall dive into this in Part 5.

SKILL 16: COMPOUNDING

....

As if learning about passive income wasn't enough, learning about the effects of compounding blew my mind. Prepare to be amazed.

I have experienced the effects of compounding all my life, I just didn't understand what it was at the time. It is truly a wonderful thing and I want you to understand it too and just how powerful it can be in all areas of your life.

Albert Einstein famously said:

> *"Compound interest is the most powerful force in the universe, it is the 8th wonder of the world. He who understands it, earns it; he who doesn't, pays it."*

I would add to this that it is not just interest that compounds; anything does. It is applicable to every area of your life.

Compounding

If you make tiny incremental progress in all areas of your life every day, those incremental changes will begin to compound. Progress will be very slow at first, little more than a horizontal line on a graph. Then as it gathers momentum it begins to slope up. Then in time it takes on a life of its own and goes vertical.

Let me explain how compounding can work for you financially with an indicative example which backs-up my claim that if you are young enough, even on a low income, anyone can become wealthy.

The example below is based on a property bought in the north of England for £100,000, which is realistic as of today.

Let's examine the compounding effect in action. Remember this whole time you are only saving £400 per month, which is £4800 per year.

You can expect a rental income in the region of £540 per month, so by the time you have paid the mortgage, expenses and maintenance, you will be left with a net rental income of around £400 a month or £4,800 per year in your pocket; that's the net income.

The chart below shows the effects of compounding and gives you a clear formula to achieve financial freedom.

Notes:

This formula is a worst-case scenario. I have shown the figures based on a person on low income to prove it can be done. If you are in a position to save more or put in lump sums of money, you will achieve the numbers much quicker.

The formula shown below depends on you being able to save a minimum of £400 a month from your income and reinvesting all the rental income into more property. Therefore, it relies on you being employed throughout the period.

I have taken no account of the increase in value of each property (Capital Growth) which will be very substantial over the period.

In reality, you would never buy property and leave in that much deposit. Investors use what is called the 'buy-refurbish-refinance' model, explained in detail in Skill 19. This involves refurbishing the property to add value, then refinancing the property back to 25% loan-to-value and taking out the additional equity to invest again. Therefore, in reality, you would achieve the number of properties much quicker.

	Savings This Year	Rent Profit This Year	Bank Balance to date	Houses Bought This Year	Total Houses owned to Date
Year 1	£ 4,800.00		£ 4,800.00	0	0
Year 2	£ 4,800.00		£ 9,600.00	0	0
Year 3	£ 4,800.00		£ 14,400.00	0	0
Year 4	£ 4,800.00		£ 19,200.00	0	0
Year 5	£ 4,800.00		£ 24,000.00	0	0
Year 6	£ 4,800.00		£ 28,800.00	1	1
Year 7	£ 4,800.00	£ 4,800.00	£ 9,900.00	0	1
Year 8	£ 4,800.00	£ 4,800.00	£ 19,500.00	0	1
Year 9	£ 4,800.00	£ 4,800.00	£ 29,100.00	1	2
Year 10	£ 4,800.00	£ 9,600.00	£ 15,000.00	0	2
Year 11	£ 4,800.00	£ 9,600.00	£ 29,400.00	1	3
Year 12	£ 4,800.00	£ 14,400.00	£ 20,100.00	0	3
Year 13	£ 4,800.00	£ 14,400.00	£ 39,300.00	1	4
Year 14	£ 4,800.00	£ 19,200.00	£ 34,800.00	1	5
Year 15	£ 4,800.00	£ 24,000.00	£ 35,100.00	1	6
Year 16	£ 4,800.00	£ 28,800.00	£ 40,200.00	1	7
Year 17	£ 4,800.00	£ 33,600.00	£ 50,100.00	1	8
Year 18	£ 4,800.00	£ 38,400.00	£ 64,800.00	2	10
Year 19	£ 4,800.00	£ 48,000.00	£ 60,600.00	2	12
Year 20	£ 4,800.00	£ 57,600.00	£ 66,000.00	2	14
Year 21	£ 4,800.00	£ 67,200.00	£ 81,000.00	2	16
Year 22	£ 4,800.00	£ 76,800.00	£ 105,600.00	3	19
Year 23	£ 4,800.00	£ 91,200.00	£ 116,100.00	4	23
Year 24	£ 4,800.00	£ 110,400.00	£ 117,300.00	4	27
Year 25	£ 4,800.00	£ 129,600.00	£ 137,700.00	4	31
Year 26	£ 4,800.00	£ 148,800.00	£ 177,300.00	6	37
Year 27	£ 4,800.00	£ 177,600.00	£ 188,700.00	6	43
Year 28	£ 4,800.00	£ 206,400.00	£ 228,900.00	8	51
Year 29	£ 4,800.00	£ 244,800.00	£ 250,500.00	8	59
Year 30	£ 4,800.00	£ 283,200.00	£ 310,500.00	10	69
		£ 331,200.00			

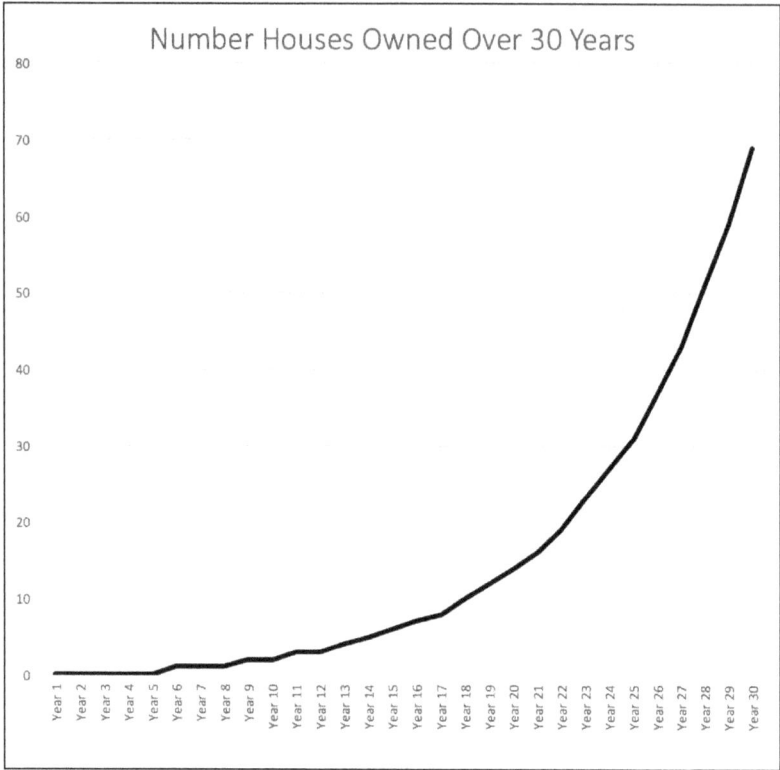

Number Houses Owned Over 30 Years

Based On:

- Making £400 a month or £4800 a year rent.
- Savings from wages £400 a month or £4800 a year.
- Deposit of £25,000 per house.
- Costs £3,500 per house. (Stamp Duty and Fees.)

As you can see it takes between five and six years of hard discipline saving £400 a month to be in a position to afford the £28,500 deposit to buy your first property. This is the hard part.

Then, because you can now add the £400 rent to your £400 savings it only takes two-three years of saving to afford your second property. By year nine you have two houses.

That might not sound a lot, but because you can now add the rent from two houses to your savings, it only takes one-two years to afford property number three.

Then by year 15 you own six houses.

In years 16 to 20 you can buy another eight houses, taking you to 14 in total. You now have 14 times £4,800 a year rent coming in, that's £67,200 a year for the rest of your life. You have achieved this in only 20 years saving only £400 a month.

If you started at age 20, you are now at the grand old age of forty. You could stop there and never work another day in your life. But if you chose to continue, things start to get really interesting.

Because of the effects of compounding, between years 20 to 25 you can buy 17 houses. Taking you to 31 houses with an income of £148,800. You could stop here if you wish.

But you don't stop, you are only 45. You carry-on saving just £400 a month, which is nothing by that time, for a further five years until you are 50 and using the rent to buy even more houses.

If you choose to continue until you are a very young 50, with the effect of compounding, believe it or not, you could be buying ten houses that year and you will own 69 houses with a net income of £331,200 a year.

We haven't even spoken about the massive amount of capital growth those 69 properties will have undergone. You are a millionaire. You have a property portfolio worth over £10 million and your equity (cash) in those properties will be well over £2.5 million.

Your property portfolio is now self-sustaining. All you need to do is find a good team to source houses, buy them and rent them out. You have achieved complete financial freedom and have the choice to keep going, or stop and enjoy the income. If you keep going, the rate of growth will be astonishing.

You will be leaving a serious legacy for your children and grandchildren.

Gob-smacked? I know I was. All it takes is £400 a month, reinvesting your rental income and a whole lot of dedication to your cause.

This is the very model we as a family are using to make us all financially free.

Practicalities

Now I'm not saying this is going to be easy, far from it. I'm sure you can appreciate that earning £331,000 plus a year net passive income in your lifetime could never be easy.

Your biggest problem will be finding enough property to buy. It will take a big effort on your part to buy that many properties, but, like anything else, your skills and network will compound too and every property you buy will give you more experience until it becomes second nature. Trust me, it's not that hard; I can say that with one-hundred percent conviction, because as I said, this is exactly what my family are doing.

Effects of compounding your financial education

Please don't think of compounding just in terms of money. Anything carried out consistently over a long period will give you positive incremental changes and eventually compound.

One of the most important things you can do to start your financial freedom journey, is to educate yourself. Your financial education is critical if you intend to build wealth. If done every day over a sustained period you will soon become proficient and then expert in your field.

Malcolm Gladwell in his 2008 book Outliers, suggested that anyone practising anything for 10,000 hours will be an expert in that field. He and others have argued that genius is not born, but learned through dedicated practice.

Take my son Luke, now aged 24. He left school at 16 and started working in admin for our building company. He got interested in property and signed up for a one year property investment class and read lots of books on the subject.

With this information, he developed his financial freedom plan, which is still on the wall over his desk in his bedroom. He didn't earn that much money as a trainee, but most of what he did earn he saved to buy a buy-to-let property using exactly the same system as above.

He plans to be financially free by age 35 and is on-track to achieve that. He already owns two BTLs, giving him an income of over £900 per month. The effect of all that study and all that saving is beginning to have a really positive effect on Luke's life and I have no doubt that if he keeps on going he will achieve his goal with no assistance from me, other than guidance and encouragement.

One of Luke's favourite books on property investing is *Property Investing* by Rob Dix. A deep-dive into the do's and don'ts of buying and renting property.

Luke is proof that almost anyone can do it if they have the determination to do positive things every day and let the effects of compounding work its magic.

I would urge you to attend to the following areas in your life and make incremental change for the better every day:

Generally:

- Good food.
- Exercise.
- Main relationships in your life.

Financial:

- Learn about money and investing.
- Choose your investment strategy and become an expert.

If you apply positive incremental attention to the areas above in your life every day, over the long-term your life will improve beyond your wildest dreams.

Becoming you?

In his book Atomic Habits, James Clear suggests that the little things we do habitually make us who we are and who others perceive us to be. If you want to be known as an expert at investing in gold and silver, study that. If you want to be the go-to person for buying houses, study that. The perception people have of you is entirely your own doing and you can shape and build that perception every day by your habits, good or bad.

I've seen this in action for myself. My youngest son Alex, now 19, started with the firm at age 16. He went into our property side and took to it like a duck to water. To say he studies would be an understatement. Alex studies every week night.

All this has meant that from the age of 16 until 19, Alex gained the skills to manage a large property portfolio single handed. That is some achievement. If the family want to know about property, Alex is our go-to person, even at his age. He has built that knowledge himself and now the perception others have of him is that he is the property expert. The compounded effect of all that study has been phenomenal.

The same, of course, can work in reverse. You could be known for being an expert at watching Netflix series. Sadly, too many of the population fall into that category.

If you want further reading on compounding, *The Slight Edge* by Jeff Olsen is a good place to start.

SKILL 17: LEVERAGE

I hope by this stage you are beginning to see the potential you have and are getting excited about the prospect of getting started. The next principle will come in very useful.

Just like compounding, this is another great concept to help you build your wealth and is fairly simple to understand.

Leveraging in investment terms means using other people's money, OPM, to help you get into a deal. Using leverage is pretty much essential if you want to build wealth.

An example of how leveraging would be used in a property deal is as follows:

In the previous example, we used the bank's money to buy houses costing £100,000 each, putting in a deposit of £25,000. This means you leveraged the bank's money to buy the house. You turned your £25,000 into £100,000 to buy the house to enable you to get in the deal and earn cash flow. No leverage, no house.

This is also a good example of the good debt we discussed previously in Skill 13.

Some stocks and share deals work in the same way, as we shall see in Skill 21.

Leveraging in business

Soon after I took over my dad's company, I did a deal that involved leverage to help the business grow, although, I didn't understand that it was leveraging at the time.

I wanted to set up a joinery shop as we were outsourcing our joinery. I had some money in the bank but not enough to buy a property. I called my bank to ask for a loan.

They asked for all sorts of security, including a personal guarantee and a charge over my home; after I agreed, they lent me the money.

The debt was to be paid back over a ten-year period on a capital and interest loan (Skill 28). I found a property, set up a joinery shop and we began trading.

The business thankfully was profitable and with the profit we were able to make our monthly repayment to the bank with some profit left over. That's leveraging someone else's money to earn profit.

If you intend to become an investor, you need to get your head around the concept of using other people's money, to leverage up. But there is one caveat. You need to use leverage safely, leaving yourself a good amount of margin for error.

In the example above, let us assume that you borrowed 90% of the asking price instead of 75%. You borrow £90,000 and put in only £10,000 deposit.

If interest rates went up only two or three percent and you are out of your fixed interest rate period, your repayments could go up to say £520 but your rent would still be £500. You are in big trouble because you cannot cover your mortgage. This is what happened in 2008.

Leverage-up by all means, but build in a safe margin of error.

PART 5: INVESTING

Everything so far has been preparing you for Part 5. Which is really the meat of the book, where you learn the actual investment strategies.

As we go through, I want you to start thinking about what strategy you would feel comfortable with. Everyone develops a favourite or favourites.

By the end of Part 5 you will have a good understanding of the following types of investment and how you can start investing.

18. Investment Principles
19. Investing in Rental Property
20. Investing in Gold and Silver
21. Investing in the Stock Market
22. Digital Currencies
23. Passive Income and Capital Growth
24. Starting a Business

SKILL 18: INVESTMENT PRINCIPLES

What sort of person you are and your life experiences will determine what you feel comfortable investing in. We are all different.

Before we discuss the specific investment strategies we need to set your investment parameters. These are a set of 'guiding principles' that become your 'rules of investing'. They guide you and help you to decide quickly whether a deal is right for you.

Approach to investing

Every investor has their own approach and feels differently about different investment classes. What seems risky to one person seems like a great deal to another. Some love gold, some would never buy gold. It's all personal choice. As you begin to understand the various types of investment we discuss here, hopefully one or two will resonate with you, just like property, gold and silver did with me.

I remember my old property mentor telling me his standard reply when someone used to tell him, "it's impossible to find a property deal in this town". He would answer, "impossible for you maybe, but not me". He could say that because he was very experienced in property and could sniff a deal a mile away. His various life-skills meant that property was the natural choice for him. Being a former builder, it felt right for me too.

It's not only the type of investment that people view differently, but how they view risk. One investor may put 50% of her cash into gold and 50% into stocks. Another only 10% in gold. This is a reflection of how different people view the same investment class at that time, and we all have different views.

Some investors stick to one type of investment that they feel comfortable in, some have multiple types of investment. Some constantly move their cash around depending on how they feel about the future of certain markets. Some investors are risk taking and some risk averse.

You can see that there are many variables and in time you need to work out what feels best for you.

Some aspects of your personal preferences will be apparent instantly. For example, we all have a good idea of how much risk we are comfortable with. But others such as, how many investments classes to be involved with, may take longer for you to understand as you build up your experience.

Over time your 'personal investment profile' will become apparent, and these will be your guiding principles.

It took us a while to understand our investment preferences as a family, which are as follows:

Our investment principles

Generally speaking we are careful investors, we definitely err on the side of caution. We assess the likely outcome of our investments from all angles with a fine-toothed-comb, before we part with our money. Or rather, Luke does. Our model is as follows:

Business

We have a family construction business which year-on-year puts a certain amount of its profits into investments. We leave a healthy amount in the business, as we want to keep the golden goose healthy. We are paranoid about service as we see it as a multi-generational firm and our reputation is everything.

Property

We use the money from our business to buy one, two and three-bedroom family homes in the Midlands, near hospitals, schools, shops or factories. The properties must have parking and good transport links. Our properties have to be no more than 25 years old and freehold only.

Most of our available cash goes into properties. Our properties have to return at least £400 a month net income.

We also buy good quality commercial units with long leases in very good areas.

Gold, Silver and Stocks

Approximately 2% of our available cash goes into gold and silver, and 2% into company stocks.

Developments

This is our most risky strategy and the closest we come to speculation. Occasionally, we buy office blocks and convert them into one or two bed flats, or new build houses, then rent them out. You can make or lose a lot of money on developments and many people lose money. The only reason we go anywhere near developments is because our main business is construction. But they are certainly not for the inexperienced.

Financial education

Financial education has to be one of your principles. I say has to, because it is unlikely that you'll succeed without the required knowledge. But reading this book is a great start.

In the early days, your financial education should take priority over all else apart from work; that's how important it is.

Reading, listening to audio books and going on courses should become a way of life in the early days. Cram in as much knowledge as you can.

I feel a lack of discipline in this area is one of the main reasons people fail to progress. We all instinctively move away from pain and toward comfort, and giving up the comfort of telly to read a financial book or listen to a Brandnewtube is painful to some people, but it's a question of priorities.

Since I've been on this journey, my life habits have totally changed. I was that person in my younger day watching EastEnders, or Dead Enders as we call it, and Procrastination Street. Now I haven't watched telly for years and nothing would make me go back. The thought of listening to the propaganda on the Bad-News at Ten is scary to me. The odd Netflix on a Friday or Saturday is enough for me.

It's the same for my sons. No telly at all apart from weekends. Weekdays the computer is out, and its knowledge and planning time.

Most people just would not be bothered to build such a lifestyle, but then most people struggle for money. Perhaps you can begin to understand why not many people become wealthy.

Investment money and living money

If you are going to achieve the wealth plan set out in Skill 14, you are going to have to be disciplined with your money, so a principle has to be to prioritise saving.

A good way of doing this is to separate your bank accounts. Your current account for living expenses and a savings account for investment money, the money that is going to make you wealthy.

Start out with an amount of money you feel it will be safe to save every month and put it into a separate bank account; call this account, My Financial Freedom Account as a constant reminder. Put the money in religiously by standing order from your current account and do not touch the money, ever, for anything other than investing. Not for a holiday, not if you fall short of anything. Find another way to cover these expenses, like working late or taking another job.

Think of the financial freedom money as someone else's money, money that you have to pay first. Remember investment Rule 2: Pay Yourself First.

As we have discussed in Skill 3, be the best employee in the firm, get in early, stay late, do all you can to get a pay rise and make sure you ask for it. As a long-standing employer, I can tell you there are not many dedicated staff around and those that are get paid the most; be that person. The more you earn the more you can save and the faster invest.

Strong purpose

People who build something meaningful are generally those who for some reason have a strong drive to achieve their goal. In some cases, the driving force is not even known to themselves. For these people, failure doesn't seem to be an option. A force such as this can drive a person through the difficult times and help them achieve their goal.

I mentor such a person; his name is Adam and he is 28. Adam has worked his way from less than nothing to building two property-based businesses. One employs five staff and manages a few hundred properties, the other converts houses into separate bed apartments.

There is no doubt in my mind that Adam will become very wealthy. Apart from my own sons, I have never met such a driven person. He tells me he never watches telly either, too busy studying.

I asked him to write a few words about why he is so driven to help you understand such people.

This is what he wrote:

"I grew up with three brothers, raised single headedly by my incredible mum, who is disabled and suffers constant chronic pain. We were all abandoned by my drug addict father when I was four.

I had a hard time in school following the structure and authority style. This is where my dislike of authority started and this quickly followed me into the workplace.

When I started working, paying bills and living in my own apartment, I quickly realised how much of a struggle most people have to get by and try and live life day-to-day due to being restricted by finances. All while working jobs I always grew to hate and begrudged attending. It gave me an entirely new perspective on my upbringing and it hit me how hard my mum must have struggled which at the time I couldn't see.

I wanted to be totally free to live life to the fullest and to me, not being restricted by anything or anyone is exactly that. Initially, the drive was to be able to give my family the life they deserve and for me to love my job.

I quickly realised there was more to it than I first anticipated. Hitting my goals not only fulfils my need for constant growth, it also gives me certainty of my future, significance and brings variety into my life. The ability to give back and contribute to better other people's lives in so many different ways fulfils my need for contribution and connection. Being an entrepreneur hits every human need we have as human beings.

I feel truly alive when I'm creating and designing my businesses that all started from just an idea and belief in myself."

Adam Cooper, Freedom Homes

We sometimes see this type of drive in people who have been persecuted. Or perhaps in war-time where the common goal is survival. Or perhaps first-generation immigrants who are driven by a survival instinct to thrive in a foreign land.

I didn't understand why I was driven in my younger life until I did a psychology course when I was 40. It was a Neuro Linguistic Programming (NLP) course and the tutor was probing us, asking the simple question, "why do you do what you do?".

I thought about it for a minute and as I began to realise why, I began to well-up with emotion and then broke down.

For the first time in my life it hit me that all that study, all those weekends with my head in a book, all that compulsive drive to achieve, was all to please my dad.

My dad isn't the type to say well done or pat you on the back. He is a tough East Ender and his relationship with his often-absent father was very strained to say the least. I think that's how he formed his perception of father-son relationships and I think he thought I saw him as he saw his own father.

Needless to say, from a very early age my constant drive for my father's approval, coupled with his unwillingness to show approval, led me to be obsessed with achievement in anything I did, putting it above all else in my life.

I mentioned this to him one day, and he said, "Well, it made you the man you are, didn't it?" I had to smile.

I'm sure everyone who has picked up this book has their own story as to why they feel the need to achieve more, whether they realise it or not. The important thing is that there has to be some degree of drive, because you will certainly need to do extraordinary things out of your comfort zone on your journey to wealth.

One of the big obstacles we all have these days is that we all live in relative comfort and this can be a disadvantage. I discuss this with my sons often. They were brought up in relative comfort: a nice house, good food, security, jobs etc. We all have that to a greater or lesser degree in this country, so the question has to be asked, why should we bother to strive for more?

The answer is that you don't have to. You can sit back and do nothing, at least while in your parents' care. But that won't last forever and you will be out in the big scary world having to fend for yourself.

But even then, like most of the population you could settle for a regular 9-5 job, or welfare, a small house with small garden, average car and two weeks' holiday a year. Then work until retirement age or beyond.

There is nothing wrong with that at all, it's how most of the population live; and the reason is that evolution has instilled in us that we should go toward comfort and away from pain. For seeking out pain, like studying for years on end, taking massive action out of your comfort zone, lying awake at night because you have to confront a difficult situation in the morning. Going without, saving instead of spending, and being the odd-one-out would be counter intuitive; that is, going toward pain.

But it is only on the edge of our comfort zone that the magic happens.

At the end of the day, it is your personal choice, but if your purpose isn't strong enough, the likelihood is you'll give up.

If a common drive exists within a group of people, say in a family business, then the sky is the limit.

Goal setting

A mentee of mine keeps telling me that he will be financially free by the age of 35; it's a big thing for him and I think he will.

I say to him, "But what are you going to do after that, you will still be very young and need a purpose." Because we all still need a purpose in life, even if we are financially free.

I'm not saying do not plan and set goals – goal setting is essential. But don't look at the goal as the end, look at it as a milestone. If you look at the goal as the end and you achieve your goal, you will lose your purpose. Without a purpose, trust me, life is unbearable.

It's not the end that is important, it is every day of your awesome journey. Please trust me when I say, however hard you think it is at the time, you will long for those days back again if they are taken away. The journey is everything, so find contentment in that.

Quick wins – gambling and speculation

There will be times throughout your investment career when you will come across people perhaps on YouTube, in the press or even at the pub (when they open), telling you about the next exciting deal.

The quick bucks that can be made and the amazing investment that will change your life. Please be very cautious. There are hundreds of people and organisations out there whose aim is to sign you up to the next fantastic deal designed to relieve you of your money.

I've been there. The wife of a client worked for a time-share company selling shares in a property in Spain. The numbers looked good, I couldn't find any reason not to invest and I was getting pressure to do so from my then other half.

There was only one reason I didn't invest in the end. The property was abroad. One of my investment principles is to never invest abroad. It's not my thing. It's hard enough to keep up with the laws here in the UK, let alone Spain. To me this would have been speculation and, as an investor, I never speculate.

Hundreds of thousands of speculators lost everything in 2008. If you gamble with your hard-earned money you could well lose too. Only invest your money when you have dotted every I and crossed every T. I would urge you to develop this careful approach to your investments. There is really only one way to build solid wealth and that is slowly and steadily, building your assets with hardly any risk of losing your money.

I say hardly as there will always be some risk, but you can limit risk by going over and over the details and the figures, and project these forwards.

My old property mentor questioned me when I told him I was thinking of developing a block of flats; he said the reason he buys small houses in urban areas is that they rent every day of the week, there is no risk. He said he is an investor not a gambler. I doubted that at the time and thought it was a bit boring buying little houses. I wanted the sexy big deals, but now I know he was right.

I did buy the office block and converted it into eight flats. It took eighteen months and cost over £500,000. It was a nightmare from start to finish. For that money, we could have bought eight three-bed houses with no hassle or stress, in less than half the time. They would have cash-flowed more too.

If you are ever presented with a great deal and you really want to get in, then that is ok, but only invest a small portion of your money into the deal, an amount you can afford to lose. But remember, speculation is gambling not investing.

> ### RULE 4:
>
> # ONLY SPECULATE WITH MONEY YOU CAN AFFORD TO LOSE.

Diversification

Means to invest in more than one investment type. Is it important to diversify in investing? I say no, some say yes; it's back to personal choice again.

Some people feel it's important to spread the risk. If you only invest in one investment class and that takes a nosedive, you'll have lost everything. Take housing, for example. If you were an investor in 2007 and the only investments you had were rental properties, you could have been in real trouble. If you'd had some gold and silver, which tends to go up when house prices drop, then you could have 'hedged' your portfolio and not lost as much money.

Some investors believe that it is not good to diversify, as you can become a jack of all trades and master of none. These investors think you should pick an investment class that you feel comfortable in and get really good at it.

In 2008, had you been in property alone, but had a very low loan-to-value, say, 50%, you would have ridden out the property crash and may even have had enough funds to pick up some cheap property as the prices crashed.

I have to say that having invested in several investment classes, I do feel that it is preferable to get really good at one investment class. Ours is property. We also invest in gold and silver, stocks and land, but only for fun. Most of our money is in property. Why? Because it provides a return and generally increases in value; it's a tangible thing you can touch and feel. Also, nearly all the investors I know and good business people have property. For us, other strategies are just for fun with money we can afford to lose.

My advice is to pick the strategy you feel comfortable with and become an expert in your field.

Uncertain times

One principle which is relevant to the pandemic and the catastrophic financial disaster it is leaving in its wake. Not to mention destroying small businesses and many jobs.

If ever there were a time to learn about money it is now. We are living in an extraordinarily uncertain time in history and although we should hope for the best, we should plan for the worst.

At the time of writing, only a year ago the future was clear. But now following recent events most people's financial futures are very uncertain. If this isn't enough to give you the drive to take action, I don't know what is.

They say in every financial crash there are some people who get very wealthy. None of us know what is going to transpire in the next decade but there is one thing for sure. A few people are going to make a lot of money. You have the opportunity to turn this uncertainty to your advantage. By developing your education and then taking action, you could secure yours and your family's futures.

Giving back

To me, this is one of the main principles you should follow in life, not only in investing. It's not tangible like some of the other principles, it's very subtle but has been very significant in my life.

Throughout life I have found almost without fail that if you do something for someone unconditionally, they will want to do something equal or even bigger for you in return. In fact, I attribute much of my success to this principle.

I don't know exactly why it works. I feel perhaps it is an inherent trait in humans to want to help someone who has helped them. I certainly feel that way when someone help me.

But for the universe to work its magic, someone has to go first. Let that person be you. Make a habit of giving to others of your time and your knowledge. It will come back to you many times over.

It's one of my principles in life, which extends to the way I invest. Do something for someone for no reward and see what happens.

Gut feeling

Lastly. Please do not overlook the way you feel inside about the deal. Your gut feeling is everything.

Remember, it's taken human beings millions of years to develop their fear instinct, it's there for a reason, to protect you and it can be relied on. If it doesn't feel right, like anything in life, don't do it, whatever the numbers say. But on the other hand, if it does feel right, go for it with all your heart.

SKILL 19:
INVESTING IN RENTAL PROPERTY

I have written more about buying property than any other subject, as experience has taught me it is of interest to most people. Also, I am biased, I love it. I feel that property is the best investment for the average person as it's something we can all understand.

There is a lot to write about property investing and I've given you a good amount of detail here. In fact, a seven-point plan below which I believe is most of what you would need to know to get started.

It's fair to say that rental property has changed my life and it will change my family's for generations to come.

As we've seen in Skill 14, Passive Income, investing in property can be a very profitable strategy, but I don't want you to think it's easy; nothing in this book is easy, it requires a lot of hard work up-front and requires you to save for a deposit. If you are on a low wage, it could take several years to save enough.

I feel I should reiterate the last paragraph, because I don't want you to miss the point. Buying, refurbishing and renting property is not easy, it's bloody hard work and takes an enormous amount of effort and money before you get a penny in return. But don't be put-off, when it's rented out, it's amazing.

When I first got into property, I thought the time, money and the effort involved in finding a house, getting a mortgage, refurbishing and finding a good tenant was astonishing, and for very little return.

For example, if you bought a house in the North of England for £100,000, you would need in the region of £28,500 for deposit, stamp duty and solicitor's fees. The mortgage on that house would probably cost you £150 per month and the property would probably rent for £550-600 per month. That would be a net profit of £425 per month less money for annual maintenance. You'd be left with around £400 per month in your pocket.

It cost £28,500 of your hard earned saved up cash and six to eight months' work to get a measly £400 a month. That might not seem a lot, but let's put that into perspective.

If we take our rent of £400 per month and times that by 12 months, we get £4,800 per year rent. Not bad for one property.

Also, if we divide £30,000 by £4,800 we get 5.9. That means in nearly six years we would have paid back our initial outlay, and the rent after that point is infinite profit, or in other words, money for nothing.

As my old property mentor used to say, "it just drops into your bank every month", and believe me it does.

Looked at another way, if we divide £4,800 by £28,500 and times by 100, we get 16.8%. This is the return on our investment, or ROI. At the moment banks are offering virtually zero percent interest on savings.

You can understand why people like property.

The other thing about property is that most people can understand how the process works and so can get into the market easily. But you have to be careful – in my experience, many people who buy investment property dive-in without really knowing what they are doing. It is nothing like buying your own house.

As an investor, you need to be so much more sophisticated than the average buyer. There is so much to consider that could mean the difference between you making good money for as long as you own the property, or getting your property wrecked and losing your savings.

To make sure that doesn't happen, I've set out a seven-step guide for you to follow to buy rental property, and the first thing you need to think about is where in the country is the right place for you to buy.

7 STEP PROPERTY INVESTMENT PLAN

Step 1. Investment area

Not many people even consider this. If the house looks good, they just buy. No. Before you do anything, you need to decide on location. Investors refer to the location in which they buy their houses as their 'investment area'.

When it comes to investment areas, new investors often have no idea where to start. I can remember taking months to decide where to buy. I drove up and down motorways and stayed in many Northern and Sothern towns in England, meeting estate and letting agents, and I viewed tens of properties.

It became quite depressing in the end, driving around these strange places and staying in some real dives. It was all made worse because I was looking at lower end properties and I found out these were located in some really rough areas. I became very despondent.

I remember one morning an estate agent driving us around to see a terraced house in Doncaster, just like the ones on Coronation Street. When we arrived, there was a car burned-out and crashed into the corner of the end terraced property we were supposed to be viewing. We decided not to view. In fact, we decided to leave Doncaster.

As the weeks passed, I began to get a gut feeling that these far-away places were not for me. I was looking at a four-five-hour drive from Cambridge where I live. So, I eventually made the decision my investment area would have to be more local.

Around that time, I employed a property mentor and he told me how to work out what area would work best for my circumstances.

There are three things you can ask yourself which will help you decide where to invest. These are:

- Do I want capital growth or yield from the property?
- Am I going to be a hands-on or hands-off investor?
- Is there demand?

Growth or yield?

To reiterate, growth means the property going up in value, yield means how much rent you get.

Let's assume the main requirement at your stage of life is income. Then the amount of rent you get is the most important thing. This will influence where you buy. We have already discussed that generally in the UK Northern property is cheaper than Sothern property, but rents are not much different. In this case you may choose to buy a house up North, as we East Enders call it. Even better if you already live up-north.

Alternatively, you may value capital appreciation over cash flow, so you may want to buy in a location to maximize growth, probably the South East, or even better my area, Cambridge; massive capital growth.

Hands-On or Hands-Off

There are several types of investor. Those which are professional landlords who do this as a job. These are very hands on.

Then you have people who have certain skills who want to carry out some of the tasks, like doing any improvement work to the property, themselves, or perhaps managing a builder. If this is you, you may want to be closer to your properties to cut down journey time. In the industry, we recommend within an hour.

Or perhaps you are a high-income earner and want nothing to do with the process. You would prefer to give your money to a professional who will source, refurbish, find a tenant and manage the property for you for a fee.

The answer to all these questions will bring you nearer to your investment area.

Demand

It is critical that you understand demand.

While answering the above questions will bring you closer to your area, there is a big but. Once you have shortlisted, say, three towns, you 'must' check on the demand in the area. You can buy the cheapest property in the world, but if no one wants to rent it, it will sit there costing you money.

You can check demand in two ways. Use Rightmove to see how many properties are for sale in your price range and type, and then go to a site like Spare Room and check on how many people are looking to rent those properties. The more demand, the better.

I had a property on the market for three months once and was concerned that it would never rent. My old letting agent reassured me and said, "they all rent in the end", and in my experience, he was right; there is someone for every property, eventually, because there is more demand than supply, and demand is still growing.

The second thing you can do once you have a shortlist of towns is go visit letting agents and ask them what demand they have for different types of property. This is by far the best way to research, you'd be wise not to miss this step as agents know their rental areas and what is in demand. If they say two beds rent the best here, then you buy two beds.

One last thought. Once you've decided on your investment area, walk the streets, get a feel for the place. You will soon develop a gut instinct as to whether the street and town is for you. Remember, you could be spending a good deal of time there in the early years so you must feel comfortable.

Step 2 – Investment strategy

Once you have decided on an investment area, you need to decide on strategy.

What is an investment strategy?

There are two parts to an investment strategy. Firstly, there are lots of different types of rental property. Houses, flats, freehold, leasehold, one bed, two beds and three beds. Flats over shops, houses converted to flats. Houses with rooms rented out individually and so on...

Each strategy, just like an investment area, will suit each individual depending on their skillset and what they feel comfortable with.

Secondly there are different ways you can set your house or flat up to rent. These range from relatively simple, like a buy-to-let, to complicated, like a serviced accommodation.

Therefore, there is a logical hierarchy of strategies and many investors feel it is best to start simple and small. Make your mistakes on property that isn't going to break the bank, like a BTL. Learn from the experience then move on to the next strategy if it feels right. Or even better, become an expert at one strategy and stick with it.

The strategies shown below are in order of difficulty. In some ways this is subjective, as what is difficult for one person is easy for another. But this is a good generalisation.

- Buy to Let
- Houses of Multiple Occupation HMO
- Serviced Accommodation SA
- Rent to Rent
- Flip
- Commercial Developments

Buy to let

This is a house or flat that you buy with the purpose of renting out to an individual, couple or family. Recognised as the entry level investment.

Relatively simple to buy through a mortgage broker with an interest only mortgage. Very similar to buying your own home. You will need 25 percent deposit, plus stamp duty.

There are many letting agents who will take on any BTL for 10-12 percent of the monthly rent.

Houses of Multiple Occupation HMO

Termed HMO in the industry, this is the next level up.

HMOs are generally larger houses that have been split into separate rooms. Some have ensuites and some are self-contained with small kitchenettes, termed studios. Rented to individuals or occasionally couples.

There are three main differences between an HMO and a BTL

- HMOs earn more rent.
- HMOs can be troublesome to manage due to the house dynamic.
- HMOs have more legislation.

While a family would rent a BTL for say £700 per month, an individual renting an HMO would pay say £400 per room with say five rooms in the house, taking the rent to £2000, potentially for the same house as the BTL.

But HMOs can be notoriously difficult and time consuming to manage if you don't know what you are doing. BTLs have one family but an HMO could have people from five families and different countries, and these dynamics sometimes cause issues, especially when the people are from different backgrounds.

For this reason, many letting agents keep away from HMOs due to the time input to manage the property effectively. Those that do will charge 15% of rent and up.

There is generally a great deal of building works required to convert the property from a single dwelling to a multi-room property. The alterations required to set-up an HMO are also vastly costlier that a BTL. In my experience and in my investment area, converting a three-bed house into a five-studio block, costs between £90,000 - £150,000.

All this said, HMOs are very popular, and if you are a hands-on investor or you can find a good local managing agent, an HMO could give you a very nice return.

If you do choose to go this route, make sure you check demand in the area, as in some areas the market is flooded. That said, as my old mate used to say, "they all rent in the end".

Serviced Accommodation (SA)

Known as SA in the industry; this is another notch-up.

Think of an SA as a mini hotel, because that's exactly what it is. Now instead of £400 per room per month, you can charge £50 per night per room, that's £1500 per month. For a four-room house that's £6000.

But don't get excited just yet. Remember, as reward goes up, so does risk. The risk with SA is void periods, periods when the rooms are not rented. This comes back to checking demand as we discussed above.

Also like hotels, you have what are known as changeovers. Where the room needs cleaning, bed linen washed and changed, sometimes daily. This is a big additional expense.

That said, SAs can work very well in the right location.

One more note. An SA is leaning toward being an operational business as well as an investment strategy, as they can take up a lot of your time.

Rent to rent (R to R)

No-money-down. You do not require a deposit for this strategy, therefore rent-to-rent can be almost a no-money-down strategy.

Believe it or not, it is possible to get rental income without owning a property. This is what's known as rent-to-rent and it's quite common among property professionals.

How does it work?

Some people are landlords not by choice but by circumstance. A parent may have left their home to their children, for example. In some cases, these 'accidental landlords' do not wish to take on the hassle of letting a property, but they still quite like the idea of some cash flow.

These are the type of people that a property investor would seek out and approach for a R to R deal.

This is similar to sub-letting, in that the investor contracts to pay the owner an amount of rent monthly over a certain time period, which could be up to five years. In return, the investor takes control of the property as if it were theirs.

The investor, being an expert, will repurpose the property and achieve more rent than they pay the owner. It's a win-win situation. But the repurposing cost money, especially if converting from a single let house to an HMO, so to say this is a no-money-down strategy is untrue, it is a not-as-much-money-down strategy, as there are set-up costs. But once set-up it's cash flow for nothing.

Find a house that is already set-up and happy days.

This strategy works extremely well, the owner being paid for a single let, while the investor could double the rent as an HMO.

This is a very good strategy for those wanting to enter the property market, who lack the funds for a deposit. Or those with the skills to convert a property themselves.

Flip

Flipping is not investing but trading for lumps of cash. Flip is the term used in industry for:

- Buy - Refurbish - Sell.

This strategy is suited to those with building skills and time, who can add value to the property by working themselves and saving the mark-up of another builder. Then putting the property back on the market to sell for a profit.

Money is required to buy the house and certain types of loan called "bridging loans" are used to loan the investor enough to buy, refurbish and sell the property.

Not recommended for the beginner, as bridging loans can be very expensive, especially if you over-run on the build and are late paying back the loan.

Commercial developments

Not for the fainthearted. A commercial development is the next step up, perhaps the ultimate step as they can be very lucrative, but only if you know what you are doing. The financing arrangements can be very complicated and specialist brokers have to be used who are very expensive.

Developments can be anything from a large house conversion to a complex new-build multi-storey building. They can be very profitable but at the same time come with a massive amount of regulation, so these are really for the professionals.

Many investors employ professional teams, architects, builders, solicitors and mortgage brokers to build on their behalf. Developments are the most speculative strategy, as the outcome is not certain due to changes in the future property market, interest rates and the economy in general. A BTL, on the other hand, will almost certainly let. It's back to our old friend, risk vs reward.

Before leaving developments, I want to be sure you have the picture regarding the complexity of these deals, because I've known some gung-ho newbie investors try a development as their first deal.

The fees alone will cost you 10% of the total cost. On a million-pound build that's £100,000 in fees. We haven't even got into bridging loan costs yet. Therefore, the margin has to be excellent on these deals. The Gross Development Value, GDV, which is the value of the property at the end of the deal, has to be known at the outset, from which all calculations are taken.

Developments, unlike BTLs, are few-and-far-between. My personal opinion: keep away from them until you are very experienced.

Tax

In recent times the government has done its best to dissuade the small investor from buying property in their personal name. But please don't be put off, as it can still be the best option if you are a lower rate taxpayer.

It's a very good idea to see an accountant before you buy a property, who will look at your circumstances and advise whether to buy the property in a limited company or personally.

Forming a limited company is very easy, you can either engage an accountant or do it yourself on-line. You will need to complete a tax return at the end of the year and the cash flow will be added to your income for tax purposes.

Regulation

There is a lot of regulation that landlords need to abide by. Also, as the strategy becomes more complex, so does the regulation. But again, please do not let this put you off. So many people do not invest for the fear they don't understand the regulation. It is not difficult and there are many sites you can go to for information.

I would always recommend that you join the National Landlord Association, NLA, who send out regular legislation updates and run training courses across the UK.

If you choose to use a letting agent, who will charge you 10% of the monthly rent, they will take care of all the regulation, but it is still a good idea to understand it yourself.

Naysayers

One last thing before we move on. When I tell people I buy rental property, their usual response is something like: don't the tenants wreck your property, or, what happens if house prices drop, or, what happens if it doesn't rent out.

Most of these people never do anything with their lives, keeping in their comfort zone, never fulfilling their potential, so don't let them bring you down.

Yes, of course there is risk. But you are not stupid. You will choose the right house in the right area, good tenants and mitigate the risk of the market dropping and remember, 'all property rents eventually'.

Do not let the naysayers put you off your dream. Go for it.

Step 3. Power team

Known in the industry as 'power team', these are the professionals that you could be dealing with on your property journey. You will definitely need to get to know estate agents and tell them your property requirements. A broker to find you a mortgage and a solicitor to carry out searches and manage the finances of the transition.

It is good to remember to source these professionals in your investment area, as they will have detailed knowledge of the housing stock which could come in very useful.

- Estate Agents
- Mortgage broker
- Solicitor
- Builder
- Letting agent
- Surveyor
- Architect
- Accountant

Step 4. Find a property

So far, I've taught you how to decide on the investment area and investment strategy. I've also explained the power team so that you can move quickly when you find a good property.

Now, and only now, are you ready to begin searching for a property. Most people rush in and do this first.

Below is a list of places you can search for a property:

- Rightmove / Zoopla
- Estate agents
- Letting agents
- Auction
- Sourcing Agents

The obvious place to start is Rigtmove and that's fine. Go to the site and set-up the necessary alerts for your preferred property type.

Online portals are essential, but I would also strongly advise you to build relationships with estate agents and letting agents in your investment area. Letting agents work with landlords and some may be selling their investment property. If you are 'in' with the agent, you could be lucky enough to get an early phone call before the property even goes to market. This is a great way to find property and the bonus is that some of these properties have tenants already in place paying good money.

One word of advice when buying investment property: the market in most areas is flooded, so if you do see a property you like on Rightmove or get a phone call from an agent, move very quickly. Be prepared to drive down to view the property within hours, or you will likely lose it to a competitor. We have lost many good properties like this, so be warned.

A word about estate agents. I've learned from experience that estate agents exaggerate all the time. My property mentor told me that if an estate agent is talking, they are lying. I have met some lovely people who are estate agents, but for the vast majority, my experience is that I have found this to be true.

One major word of warning. There's one thing estate agents dislike; that is a person who has agreed to buy a property and then backs out. They hate it for two reasons. Firstly, because they have just lost commission, and secondly because it makes them look bad to the vendor, the person selling the property. Unless you have a very good relationship with the agent and buy several houses, you will likely have lost the relationship and any future early warning phone call.

While it's important to move fast, do your homework quickly and be very sure you are going to complete on the deal before you put in an offer.

Once, we even completed on a deal we knew was a bad property, just to maintain the relationship with the agent, as we saw the long-term relationship as more important than the money lost on the deal. Another time I did back out of a deal, and we have not heard from that agent since that day.

Step 5. Making an offer

When offering on a property, skilled property investors have a more scientific approach than the average Joe, who may just offer under the asking price and hope for the best.

Investors are more interested in what return the property will give and how much cash will be tied up in the property long-term. To do this they use a formula to work out what is called their "maximum offer" or Max Offer.

Working out the max offer is really asking the question:

"how much money am I prepared to leave in this deal in the long-run?".

It can be a little tricky to understand this concept, so we'll go through it step-by-step.

Stage 1. Buying and refurbishing the house:

Let us assume you buy a run-down property for:	£80,000
The Up-Front Costs are:	
25% Deposit =	£20,000
Legal fees and assume Stamp Duty =	£4,000
Refurbishment costs =	£10,000
Therefore, the total up-front costs are:	£34,000

This is the amount of money you are going to need in the short-term to buy and refurbish the house.

Stage 2. Refinancing the house.

Because the property was refurbished it is now worth more. The investor, through the mortgage broker, finds a new mortgage to "refinance" the property and take out money, so that the deposit left in again represents 25%.

Assume after refurbishment, the property is now worth: £95,000
The deposit of 25% is returned to your bank. £23,750

Therefore, we have bought the property for £80,000 and refurbished it. It is now worth £95,000. We have re-mortgaged the property and the deposit of £23,750 comes back to us.

Therefore, the original costs were = £34,000
Less 25% cash refund from the refinance = £23,750
Balance and money left in the deal after refinance = £10,250

At this point the investor has data on which to make a decision about how much to offer. In this case, if he offers the asking price, £80,000, only £10,250 of his own money will be left in the deal.

If he is prepared to leave that amount in the deal, his maximum offer is the asking price of £80,000.

Less sophisticated investors would have to leave the original £34,000 in the deal.

This tells us that even at the asking price this property is a good deal for us. Furthermore, if you were to offer the asking price, you would probably secure the property, as the competition would probably offer below asking.

On occasion, we have even offered more than the asking price, as we know that after the refurbishment the value will have gone up considerably, and all that deposit will be coming back to us after the refinance.

This is called a Buy-Refurbish-Refinance strategy, and works very well with run-down houses.

Step 6 – The refurbishment

Assuming your offer has been accepted and you have gone through the legal process, you are now the proud owner of your first investment property.

Now you have to move quickly to refurbish the property to begin either the refinance process or renting the property. Also, the first mortgage payment will become due at the end of the following month and you will have no rent to cover that unless the property is rented.

In short, you need to get the house refurbished and on the market quickly.

There are three stages to consider getting your property in good order:

Stage 1. Preparing a schedule of work

The legal process will take from six to 12 weeks depending on how busy your solicitor is. This is valuable time to get quotes from builders.

It is a very good idea to have prepared what is known as a 'schedule of work', which is basically a list of work items you require to be done when you have completed on the property.

I made the mistake in the early days of thinking that a lick of paint would do on my rental property, but this is not the case; tenants expect a very high standard of finish. There is a lot of competition so you need to make your property stand out from the crowd.

A big tip for you that I learned the hard way. The property needs to be absolutely perfect, every handle, lock, radiator and tap checked, especially the boiler which is an expensive item. If not, your phone will not stop ringing when the tenant moves in.

Stage 2. Employing a builder

Once you've prepared the schedule of work you can call local builders to provide you a quotation, or if it's minor work, consider doing it yourself to save money for your next property.

It's a good idea to get a few quotes if you can, as prices can vary drastically depending on the builder's workload and how much they mark up the work.

When you email the schedule of work to the builder, give an approximate start date and firm this up as soon as you know your completion date. Builders get booked-up very quickly and you need to get in first.

Stage 3. Managing the work

You need to decide who will manage the work on site.

This could be you if it's a lick of paint or if you are in the industry, but if not and you are putting in new bathrooms, kitchens etc, there are a lot of Building Regulations you need to comply with, so you will need an expert. A local chartered surveyor, for example, or project manager, or at least someone in the family who is familiar with the building process.

Builders will tell you they can manage their own work, but please don't be taken in by that. This would be similar to someone marking their own exam paper – it will always be perfect.

Step 7 – Property management

Now it's getting exciting. You have a lovely new house ready for a lucky tenant. Your next task is to advertise your property to the market and find that perfect tenant who will love and look after your house.

You have two choices:

- Use a letting agent.
- Advertise it yourself.

There are advantages and disadvantages to each.

As I've said, there is a lot of regulation associated with letting a property; for this reason, when we started buying property we chose to use a letting agent to make sure we were compliant. They charged 10% of the monthly rental income plus an up-front fee to cover tenant find, credit checks and the move-in process.

We did this with the first ten properties, then my son Alex, who by that time was more experienced and familiar with the legislation than I was, set-up in-house property management systems and we took them back from the agent and managed them ourselves. Incidentally, Alex was only 19 when he was managing 30 properties and buying new ones. Young people can be truly gifted.

Agents usually advertise your property on sites like Open Rent, Rightmove, Spare Room and even Facebook. All of which can be done very easily by you.

Having been through the process of using an agent and now self-advertising and managing, I would strongly recommend you do this yourself.

The problem with using an agent is that there is a conflict of interest. The agent just wants to fill the property and get their commission; they care little about the quality of tenant, from our experience.

The agent prefers the tenant to be short-term as they will charge a new finder's fee and credit check fee. They will also never take the time to develop 'a feel' for the tenant as you would yourself.

Your goal is to find a caring tenant who will stay in your house for a very long time, look after it and pay rent on time with no hassle. Only you will care enough to find that person or family.

Whether you employ an agent or not, YOU need to interview the prospective tenant, look them in the eye and get a gut feeling for the person. This is a top tip and will save you a massive amount of grief in the long-run. It is the most important part of the whole process.

All the tenants that give us grief, are the ones inherited from our old letting agent.

I would also advocate that over time you develop a trusting relationship with your tenant by carrying out any maintenance required promptly, or even immediately.

In our experience, the tenant will want to stay with you long-term and even ask you to find them a new house if they want another bedroom, for example. This happens to us all the time.

Follow that and it will be a breeze.

SKILL 20:
INVESTING IN GOLD AND SILVER

In Skill 5 and 6, we learned that gold and silver have been used for thousands of years as money and how today it has become a commodity that is a store of value over time.

In this section I am going to explain why I invest and how you can buy gold and silver. It's much easier than you would think.

Like most of the population, I'm guessing you've never given a second thought to owning gold or silver, 'bullion' as it is known. I know I hadn't until a few years ago when my son Luke, who is always open to new ways of investing, said, "look at this, Dad", and held out his hand revealing six 1oz silver coins, and so our journey into bullion began.

Before we get into the detail I need to be clear that gold or silver will never give you cash flow, unlike property. Gold isn't that sort of investment. Gold is a store of value, as we have said in Skill 6.

You remember the story of a 1oz gold coin a thousand years ago buying a toga, and today the same coin buying a suit. That is the immense power of gold. It's why wealthy families own the stuff, it's wealth preservation. There is no asset that does it better.

Why buy gold and silver?

Why would a person with money in the bank spend that money on gold or silver?

Inflation

Let us assume we have £1000 savings in the bank.

You could go out today and buy £1000 worth of goods in return for your cash. But if you left your currency in the bank for a year, then went and bought the same goods, they would have gone up in price due to inflation.

Assuming an annual inflation rate of 3%, the same goods will cost you £1030.

Put another way, your £1000 would be worth £970 in a year's time; your currency is worth less in the future.

Imagine this effect over a long period of time; year on year inflating away the value of your currency.

Gold and silver are different. They lock-in the value at the time of purchase, so at any time in the future you will usually be able to buy the same goods with the same amount of gold or silver. Of course, like any commodity there are ups and downs, but over the long-term gold and silver have maintained their value.

Currency supply

Another way, perhaps the main way currency becomes worth less, is through currency supply; the more currency in circulation the less it is worth.

Banks are continuously typing more currency into existence through the fractional reserve system (Skill 11), effectively stealing its value from the people.

If the economy is flooded with more currency, it pushes down the value of all the other currency. For example, if tomorrow the amount of currency in circulation doubled, your currency would be devalued by half. This is what happens when you hear that the government are printing money.

As currency devalues, gold and silver keep their value over time.

Spot Price

The 'Spot Price' of gold or silver just means today's price and it is the same all over the world. This is one of the big advantages with gold or silver in that you could buy some coin in the UK, holiday anywhere in the world, and easily exchange your coin for currency. This would be very useful in a crisis situation.

Seller's margin

There is only one disadvantage I can think of with buying bullion and that is 'seller's mark-up'. Sellers make money when they sell you the bullion and also when they buy it back from you. Known in investment terms as 'on the way-in and on the way-out'.

The spot price of gold at this moment is £1,342.14 per ounce. But if you bought that same ounce as a gold Sovereign, you would pay £1,420. They have marked up the spot price by nearly 6%.

It is similar on the way-out. If you were to sell the same coin ten minutes later, the price you would get would probably be around 6% under the spot price. In other words, you would have lost nearly 12%.

I wasn't overly happy about this when I first heard about it. But as someone pointed out to me, "they have to make their money somehow".

On the positive side, in time, the price of gold increases and you will make up the lost margin. Look at gold and silver as a long-term investment. Yes, you lose on the way-in, but the gold price will eventually increase and make up for the lost margin. Everything after that is profit.

How to purchase gold and silver

It's surprisingly easy to buy and sell gold and silver. It's all on-line, not much more difficult than buying something on Amazon. Companies like "GoldSilver.com" and "BullionbyPost.co.uk" are where we buy our gold from.

I'd only buy from well-known companies as you know the product will be genuine, but as always, do your due-diligence on the company. YouTube is a good place to start or Mike Maloney's book, The Guide to Investing in Gold and Silver. If you think about it, any company found sending out anything but the real thing, would be ruined by the reviews they would get.

Don't be overly concerned about someone stealing your bullion in the post. It's always delivered by a good courier like UPS or Parcelforce. It comes very securely boxed and very inconspicuous. We had some delivered when we were out once and it went to the post office. After a short panic, it turned out to be fine. The post office assistant just said the box is heavy. If it's silver it will be.

There are sometimes issues with you paying over the internet. One 1oz gold coin as of today will cost you around £1,500, so if you buy ten, that's probably a transaction that your bank will flag-up for security purposes. So be prepared for some phone calls to your bank to straighten things out.

Payments can either be made by credit or debit card, or you can ask to be invoiced for the bullion, but there is a small premium to pay if they invoice you.

One tip. Shop around when you are looking for bullion. Mark-ups vary significantly from dealer to dealer and from time to time.

What to buy

Both gold and silver have held their value over thousands of years, making them a safe haven for investors.

A 1oz gold coin costs around £1,500 today but one silver coin only costs £20. Today you'll get 75 silver coins for one gold coin. What you buy will depend on your personal circumstances and here are a few things to consider:

Weight

To put gold and silver into perspective, a "Monster Box", which is 500 x 1oz silver coins, weighs 40lbs or 18kg. Any of you who have ever lifted an 18kg dumbbell knows that is fairly heavy. That box will measure 270mm x 220mm x 100mm and be worth approximately £9,500. For the same currency, you could buy 6.7 gold coins and easily hold them in your hand.

The sheer mass and weight of the coins could influence what you buy.

Uses

People generally buy gold and silver as a hedge against currency deflation. A hedge means reducing the risk of an investment. People who buy gold and silver feel that it is safer than some other investments or holding money in the bank.

While both gold and silver are considered a store of value, they each have other uses which are recognised as a further hedge by investors. Gold's other main use is as jewellery, although it is used in small amounts in other industries. Silver, on the other hand, has multiple uses in industry, and for this reason even if its price as a commodity drops, it will still have a strong value to industry.

Coins or bars

Opinions vary but most experts would encourage you to start with gold or silver coins, which come in many sizes and weights. Start with coins like the American Eagle, Silver Britannia, Australian Kangaroo and the Canadian Maple. These coins are easily recognised by investors and you'll have no problem selling. Our Royal Mint mints coins for over 80 countries and any Royal Mint coin would be a good buy.

Bars are also a reliable investment and can sometimes be slightly cheaper. It's really up to the investor, but in my opinion bars are less flexible than coins. It's difficult to break a bar in half to pay for something in a crisis, so coins give more flexibility in this respect.

Storing your bullion

Before you begin investing in gold and silver, and I suggest you do, take a moment to consider where you are going to stash your bullion.

If you invest over the long-term and buy silver, you'll have some heavy boxes to deal with and you'll need space to store them. Gold will be much easier size-wise, but is much more valuable and this brings with it the obvious security issues.

Good on-line dealers will offer secure storage facilities at reasonable prices, which is ok, but you don't have the shiny stuff in your possession when you need it. If you are in a position to buy a lot of bullion, then storage at one of the many secure facilities will be a must. Alternatively, you could buy a safe, bury your bullion or hide it.

If you do buy bullion there is one rule. Do not tell anyone about your bullion. News travels fast and if it gets to the wrong ears, you or your family could find yourselves in trouble. We made the decision when writing this book to use an off-site storage facility for our gold and silver, which is recommended.

Civil Unrest

We live in unprecedented times. There is civil unrest all over the world, most of which is emotionally charged by economic dissatisfaction or political interference in the day-to-day lives of the people, as seen by the pandemic.

We in the UK have been relatively lucky since World War Two to have been in a period of relative peace. But since 2008 and the housing crash the world has been going through another financial crisis which many are saying is going to be worse than any other we have experienced in recent history.

Roughly every 75 years going back in time, there has been a global financial reset and a new currency. We are 76 years from the last one in 1944, called 'The Bretton Woods System'.

Many experts believe we are now going through a new global economic and currency reset and it is not clear what the new system will be.

With big change comes fear, with fear comes disorder. This is a time to prepare for what could happen and protect your family. As the saying goes, "hope for the best but plan for the worst".

You can find out much more about this from Simon Dixon who can be found on "BanktotheFuture.com" or on his YouTube channel.

In such times when a new currency is being rolled out to the people, silver has proven very useful over the years and can be used as currency to buy goods and services, as can gold. Silver is particularly useful as currency because the value of a coin is much less than gold and can buy day-to-day goods. This could enable you to buy goods until the new currency is accepted by the people, anywhere in the world, as the 'spot price', which is the global price, is the same everywhere.

SKILL 21:
INVESTING IN THE STOCK MARKET

....

For most of my life I had preconceived ideas about the stock market. I'd always thought it seemed mysterious and something other people got involved with who were in the know. How wrong I was.

A few years ago, all those preconceptions came crashing down when my then 21-year-old son Luke came home and proclaimed that he'd invested in the stock market; just like he'd done with gold and silver.

Jumping up from my chair I said, "tell me about it".

After a quick lesson, where he showed me the companies he'd bought on his iPhone, I was soon kicking myself for not learning how to invest in the stock market years ago.

Like most things, when you take the time to do some research, you find it's not that difficult, dare I say, easy. Let me just qualify that: investing in the stock market is easy; making money on the stock market is far from easy.

Our goal here is to remove the mystique around the stock market and help you understand how to invest. It's over to Luke who wrote a detailed overview of the stock market and a step-by-step guide to investing.

What is the stock market?

The dictionary defines the word 'market' as:

"A regular gathering of people for the purchase and sale of provisions, livestock and other commodities."

Put simply, the stock market or a 'Stock Exchange', is somewhere you go to buy and sell shares of companies. Companies listed on a Stock Exchange must be Public Limited Companies. There are many Stock Exchanges around the world and each Exchange 'lists' different companies. For example, if you want to buy some shares in Tesco PLC, you would visit the London Stock Exchange. Whereas if you wanted to buy Tesla PLC, you'd go to the NASDAQ Exchange.

Let's now look at shares in a bit more detail. A 'share' is a unit of ownership in a company or stock. In the context of investing, another word for 'company' is 'stock'. You can own shares in a stock, or own shares in a company, the two mean the same thing.

If I buy shares in a company, I own part of that company. For example, if a company has 100 shares and I own one of those shares, then I own 1% of that company.

Shares can go up and down in value depending on many factors such as profitability, future outlook of the industry and general supply and demand.

Money can be made by "trading' in the stock market, which means buying a share at one price, then selling it at a higher price later. Or it can be done by 'investing' in the stock market, which means to purchase shares and hold onto them for the longer term, and making an income from dividends paid to you.

Dividends

A dividend is the reward (cash flow) an investor gets for owning shares in a business, more specifically it's a share of profits paid to you the shareholder. Because it's a 'share of the profits' it goes without saying that a company can only pay a dividend if it makes a profit. For example, if I own 10 shares in ABC PLC and they announce a dividend of £3 per share, I will make £30 in dividend income.

Even if profits are plentiful, not all companies pay dividends. The decision to pay a dividend is left to the Board of Directors.

Some companies choose not to pay a dividend because they want to re-invest their accumulated profits - also known as 'Retained Earnings' back into the business. They do this to grow the business.

If you own these types of shares you may not get a dividend, but the capital value of your share is more likely to increase over time with the reinvestment of profits. Similar to Skill 19, where my dad discussed cash-flow vs capital growth when buying rental property.

Other companies are what we call 'mature'. This means they are already very large and there is little requirement to re-invest profits. Some examples include Tesco, British Telecom or British Petroleum. These companies pay a much higher dividend.

Indicies

Have you ever heard of the term FTSE 100 or S&P 500? These are what we call indices, or an 'index'. A market index is a way to categorize a range of companies by type. For example, if you're an investor in the UK looking to invest in big companies, wouldn't it be useful to know what the largest 100 companies are in the UK? That's where indices come in. In this scenario, you would look at the FTSE 100 index, which lists the top 100 companies in the UK.

THE SCHOOL LEAVER'S GUIDE TO MONEY

Here are some common indices used in the UK and American markets:

- FTSE 100 – Lists the 100 companies in the UK with the highest market capitalisation.
- FTSE 250 – Lists the next 250 companies in the UK with the highest market capitalisation after the FTSE 100.
- Dow Jones Industrial Average – A list of the largest 30 companies in the United States; this criterion is measured by editors of the Wall Street Journal as opposed to using market capitalisation.
- S&P 500 – Lists the 500 companies in the United States with the highest market capitalisation.

Diversification

The famous American investor Warren Buffet once said, "diversification is protection against ignorance". I couldn't agree more. Putting all your eggs in one basket can be a profitable option, provided you are educated and experienced in the chosen field of investment. Our main investment strategy, as you may have gathered by my dad's reference to houses, is property – he loves it because he can feel and look at it.

For now, since you're just starting out, diversification is a great tool. If you have a diversified portfolio then in the bad times you will lose less money. However, in the good times you may make less money. This is the trade-off we make for protection.

But how do we diversify in stocks?

Invest across an index

A great way to diversify is to purchase every company listed on an index. I could buy a small number of shares in every company listed on the FTSE 100. By doing this I'm protected in the event that any of those companies performs badly, because this is off-set against companies that have performed well.

Invest in opposing markets

Sometimes when one market goes down, another goes up as a result. For example, when the stock market crashes, people get scared, sell their shares, and buy into a 'safe haven'. Gold bullion is a great store of value over time and is therefore used as that safe haven, as we have seen in Skill 6 and 20.

People buying gold en masse will cause its price to rise. Meaning if you own some gold alongside your shares, while your shares will drop in value during a crash, this will be offset by the gains made in your gold holding.

This isn't an exact science but proves as an example.

Invest across sector

Sometimes a crash might affect all companies in a particular sector, for example the 'Tech Bubble' in 2000 affected all Technology companies, the Covid-19 pandemic has hit the leisure and travel industry the worst, while pharmaceutical companies are doing great. To diversify, spread your investments across different sectors.

Mutual funds

While shares are the main instrument you'll be buying, there are all sorts of financial products you could buy in the markets. One of those is called a 'Mutual Fund'.

A mutual fund is a pot of money pooled together by thousands of investors to purchase financial products. Why is a mutual fund useful?

Let's imagine you have £100 to invest. You go to the markets to purchase some investments. How much bargaining power do you think you'll have with £100? Not much.

If you have £20,000,000, your ability to get good deals is greatly improved.

This is why we have mutual funds; thousands of investors come together, pitch in their money, however big or small, and together they have much more buying power.

Below shows the basic structure of a mutual fund:

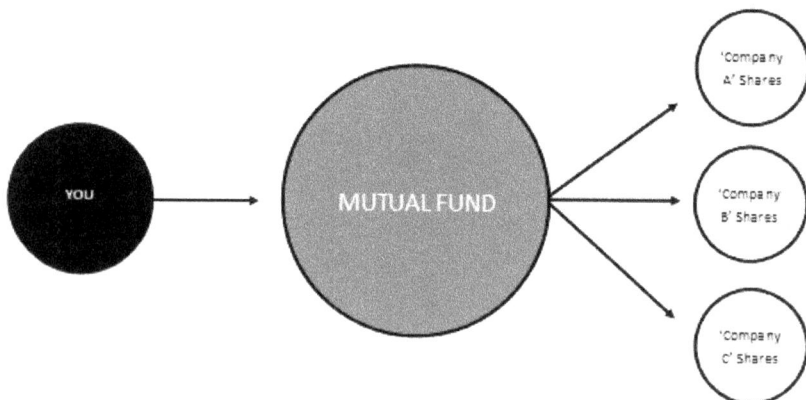

Mutual funds come in all different shapes and sizes; they also have different aims. For example, one fund may aim to purchase just FTSE 100 companies, while another buy only property investment companies.

This is why mutual funds are a great way to diversify, because instead of you buying 100 individual stocks in the FTSE 100, you could instead just buy one FTSE 100 mutual fund share. The hard work is done for you.

There are two main categories of mutual fund; these are Actively Managed Funds and Passive/Index Tracker Funds. Don't let the wordy names put you off. Let's look at these in-turn:

Active Funds

These types of funds come with a 'Professional Fund Manager'. This is a person employed to watch over the fund and ultimately help increase its returns.

The benefits of Active Funds are the possibility of higher returns and added protection in a downturn. For example, if the fund owns shares in Tesco PLC and that company crashes, then the Fund Manager will sell these shares and re-invest the money into a better performing company.

The downside to Active Funds is that the Fund Managers are expensive. Fees in an Active Fund are much higher than a Passive/ Index Tracker Fund for this reason.

Passive / Index tracker funds

These funds do not come with a Professional Fund Manager; their aim is to 'track' the performance of an Index. They do this by purchasing shares of all companies listed on a particular index in equal proportion. By doing this, the fund will track the relative performance of that index.

Therefore, if you wanted to diversify across the FTSE 100, the easiest way to do this is to buy a share of a FTSE 100 Index Tracker Mutual Fund.

The benefits of Index Trackers are reduced fees. No Fund Manager means low costs. The main disadvantage is that in a downturn you're not protected, the fund will continue to hold falling shares.

On average, over the long-term, Index Tracker Funds have performed better than Active Funds. While the Active Funds provide better protection, the increased fees inherent within them eat away at your profits over time.

There are many types of fund structures; however, this is beyond the scope of this book. If you'd like to do your own research, I've given you the name of a great book near the end of this skill, but some of the main funds are:

- Unit Trusts
- OEIC (Open Ended Investment Companies)
- ETF (Exchange Traded Funds)
- CEF (Closed Ended Funds)

Taxes

I'm not a tax advisor, this is simply the basics from my experience of investing and saving money. Seek your own professional advice.

Here's the tax you'll pay when investing in shares in the UK:

Dividend Tax

You will pay tax on dividends earned on your shares. In England, as at the time of writing, this is 7.5% in the lower tax band and 32.5% in the higher tax band. There is a £2000 dividend allowance. This means you can earn £2000 in dividend before paying tax.

Capital Gains Tax

You pay capital gains tax on the profit made from the purchase and sale transaction of a share. The rate varies based on your circumstances, so be sure to look this up.

Stamp Duty

You'll pay 0.5% Stamp Duty tax on the value of any UK shares purchase transaction. This is provided the purchase is conducted via the UK electronic settlement system 'CREST'. If you use an online app to purchase the shares this is the main method.

Stocks and shares ISA

I would always recommend investing inside a stocks and shares ISA. ISA stands for Individual Savings Account.

If you deposit your money into a stocks and shares ISA account and purchase your shares inside this, you will:

- Not have to pay any tax on dividends earned
- Not have to pay any capital gains tax on profits made on sale transactions
- Pay Stamp Duty at the usual rate.

As at July 2020, you can deposit £20,000 into a Stocks and Shares ISA per tax year.

In summary, use a Stocks and Shares ISA.

Players of the game

There are some 'players' I need to introduce to you.

Stockbroker

As an investor, you will need to open an account with a stockbroker to buy and sell shares. Many companies and stock exchanges do not allow you to deal direct, nor would you want to. You log your request with your stockbroker and they go to the market and execute the transaction for you. They then keep a log for you of what shares you own and provide you with other useful information. Some stock brokers charge fees, some don't. It all depends on the level of service they provide.

Market makers

If the stock market is a stiff, squeaky wheel, then the Market Makers are the oil. They are the people who buy the shares from you and they are the people you buy shares from. Market Makers can buy the shares from you instantly, no need to wait for another willing buyer to come along. The Market Maker will hold the shares until such time a willing buyer comes along. I like to think of them as the 'wholesalers' of the Stock Market.

Market Makers are usually financial institutions or banks and they make their money in a very specific way, the 'Bid/Offer spread'.

Let me explain this in simple terms:

If you want to buy a share, you will pay the Ask Price.

If you then decide to sell the share, you'll receive the Bid Price.

The price in the middle of these two benchmarks is known as the Mid-Price.

The difference between the Bid and Ask price is known as the Spread.

The Spread is the 'fee' investors pay to execute a transaction. This is how the Market Makers make money.

Example:

ABC PLC shares are trading at the mid-price of £100. The Market Maker's profit margin on this stock is £0.50 per share.

You pay £100.50 for one share to cover the price of the share and the Market Maker fee. The deal is done and you buy the share.

You instantly regret your purchase and go back to the market to sell your share, the price you sell the share for is £99.50. This time we're selling £100 worth of share for £0.50 less than its worth, meaning the Market Maker obtains their £0.50 profit.

Process of a buy/sell transaction

Below is a diagram of how an actual 'buy' transaction works. Examine it and then we'll go through it step by step.

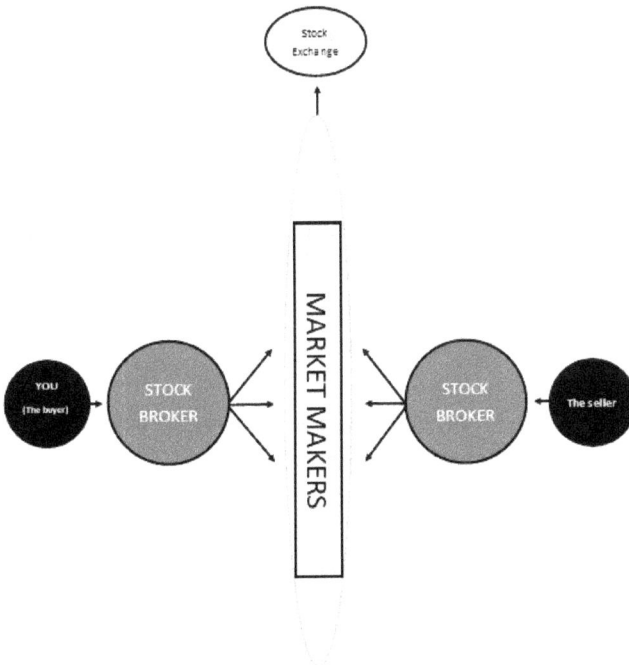

Step 1 – The seller of the shares lodges a 'sell' order with their broker; this is set at the current bid price.

Step 2 – The broker goes to the relevant Stock Exchange and consults Market Makers to 'match' the order.

Step 3 – Market Makers purchase the shares at the set price.

Step 4 – You lodge a 'buy' order with your broker. This is set at the current ask price.

Step 5 – Your broker goes to the relevant Stock Exchange and consults Market Makers to 'match' the order.

Step 6 – Market Makers sell you the shares at the set price.

If done online, this process often takes seconds because it's all computerised. You are now the proud new owner of some shares!

Step-by-step guide to buying shares

Step 1 – Get a smart phone or computer.

We'll be doing all our investing on mobile phones or computers.

Step 2 – Download the Yahoo Finance mobile app.

Yahoo Finance is what we'll use for our research and due diligence when analysing what stock to buy. It has up-to-date market news too which is very helpful.

Step 3 - Download the Trading 212 app and open a stocks and shares ISA with them.

Trading 212 is the Stockbroker that I use. Be sure not to use their CFD platform until you're experienced, only open a standard ISA account.

Trading 212 is free and quite good I think, especially for beginners. They make their money by trying to up-sell you onto their CFD platform which is chargeable, which again I urge you to stay away from if you're a newbie!

Step 4 - Deposit £100 into your Trading 212 ISA account.

Think of this £100 as your cost of education. Because you'll likely lose it. Trading 212 have a 'fake money platform' where you get a pretend £50,000 and invest this into the real market for practice.

I would recommend not bothering with this. You won't learn how to truly invest. This is because investing is 50% skill and 50% human emotion. You only gain experience on the emotion side if you use your real money.

So, go ahead and deposit £100 into Trading 212. Don't worry if you lose it, it's the price we pay for education and experience.

Step 5 - Find companies to invest in.

Trading 212 will let you search companies by all sorts of criteria; have a play around. Get used to the platform.

Find some companies you like and do a bit of research on them. Look at their financial statements, check their related news on Yahoo Finance, look at their website, find out what they do. Don't actually buy anything yet, we're just finding our feet.

Step 6 - Due Diligence.

Create a shortlist of two companies you'd actually like to invest in and check them out. The rule here is that the more due diligence you do, the better your chances of earning money. Here is the process I go through when doing due diligence:

Check the Shares Are Good Value for Money

Do this by taking the pre-tax profit of the company. Multiply this by 15. This will give you a figure. Compare this figure with the company's 'market cap' figure. If the market cap is higher, I don't buy the share.

You see, the market capitalisation figure, is the value of one share multiplied by the number of shares in existence for a company. This is what the market deems the company to be worth.

Let's assume you're a rich person looking to buy an entire company. The company in question is worth £1,000,000 but only makes £2000 per year profit.

Does that sound like a reasonable investment to you? It shouldn't. There are so many companies like this, they are the flavour of the month. Valued way more than their actual ability to make profit. When the next crash comes, unless they get some sort of break-through, they'll be the first to adjust down to their true value.

Check the debt

- Do this by taking the pre-tax profit, multiply this by three. You get a figure. If the 'Net Debt' listed on the Balance Sheet is more than this figure, I don't buy.

One of the main reasons companies go under is because the bank pulls the plug. Don't risk investing in highly leveraged companies.

Check profitability

- Check last three years' pre-tax profits. Are they rising? Good sign. Not rising? Beware.

Sector Check

- Can you see positive growth in the sector long-term? Or is it a 'typewriter company'? Soon to become extinct?

Quick News Check

- Use the Yahoo Finance app to check the news wires regarding the company. Any bad news? Does this affect your decision?

Understand the Company

- You must understand exactly what the company does and how it makes its money. You're the shareholder, after all; if you don't know then who does?

Check their website too. Does it all make sense? Would you buy from them as a customer?

Step 7 - Buy your first shares.

Once you have undertaken your due-diligence and are happy that you have two companies short-listed, buy them. Put £50 on each stock out of your £100.

Step 8 - Monitor and learn (The learning rollercoaster)

Watch how one day your £100 goes up, then down, then back up. You hear some bad news about the company and you consider selling, but then you hold your nerve. This is the 'learning rollercoaster'.

Not only are you learning how to invest, but you're learning how you react emotionally in certain market conditions. It's important we get a grasp of our emotions. If you freak out over £100, imagine the panic attack you'll have over £100,000.

Use this time, about three months, to learn, find out more about Trading 212 and practise setting a stop-loss and price alerts. Also, read books and educate yourself further on investing during this time. One book that really helped me was 'The Naked Trader' by Robbie Burns. I also joined reputable investing Facebook group too. All this while seeing how your actual money is responding to the market on a daily basis.

Step 8 – Get serious

You've finished the learning rollercoaster; I hope you enjoyed your ride?

You're now a little wiser and ready to begin investing for real. But, remember you're always learning, so don't get cocky!

So, what are you waiting for? Go ahead and deposit your investment money. Remember to repeat my due diligence process before buying. Oh, and please remember to only invest with money you can afford to lose!

SKILL 22:
INVESTING IN CRYPTOCURRENCIES

I have yet another son, Ben, to thank for this Skill. Ben did a great presentation to the family this year on Bitcoin and much of this content is Ben's.

As Bitcoin is the market leader, the remainder of the text will be around Bitcoin.

Current price at time of writing per Bitcoin is around £39,000 or $55,000.

Bitcoin is designed to bring the features of cash to the digital realm and combine them with a monetary policy that cannot be manipulated by the banks, unlike the fiat currency in use today.

Cryptocurrency is a relatively new person-to-person form of electric cash as the following quotes set out:

Cryptocurrency: "It is the newest technology
to serve the function of money".
Saifedean Ammous

Cryptocurrency is a digital form of currency, created and managed using advanced encryption techniques, known as cryptography.

Investopedia

You may be surprised, as I was, to learn that as of August 2020 there were 6,083 cryptocurrencies according to Google and the first was Bitcoin, used in January 2009.

Unlike our modern-day currency which is centrally controlled by the government and the central banks, cryptocurrencies are decentralised. There are no owners and no one controls Bitcoin, it is absolutely a peer-to-peer financial system. If you want to pay your friend or a shop in Bitcoin, the transaction will come from you directly to them. The transaction is outside of the mainstream financial system and this is very attractive to many investors and people in general.

In a centralised system such as we currently have, in order to make a transaction we ask a third party, usually a bank, to pay, and as such have 'third-party risk'. This is a concern to many investors and as we have seen in Skill 10 and 11, there is a risk of banks taking your money in a bail-in situation.

This is impossible with cryptocurrency.

Bitcoin

How does Bitcoin work?

PROOF and VERIFICATION

Bitcoin is able to work because of a system of encryption, similar to that of a text message, where the saucy picture of you gets scrambled by an encryption key; which can only be unscrambled by the intended recipient.

The process works as follows:

Step 1: You have downloaded a bitcoin wallet. This serves the same function as your bank account.

Step 2: You send your friend some Bitcoin. This transaction carries with it a 'public key encryption', which is proof of the transaction's validity.

Step 3: The transaction is verified by what are known as 'miners'.

Step 4: Once the transaction is verified, it is recorded onto the ledger, otherwise known as the blockchain.

Step 5: The blockchain is updated every 10 minutes, and every computer in the network is updated.

Bitcoin wallet

A bitcoin wallet is a computer file where a person's bitcoin is stored. It's a bitcoin bank account. A wallet can be accessed using an app or other software. The wallet also stores the public and private keys to enable 'public key encryption'.

You can go to bitcoin.org and it will talk you through a list of wallets that will suit your needs.

The network

Every balance and transaction is recorded by every other member of the network, sharing a common ledger; the blockchain.

Hacking Bitcoin at present is thought to be near impossible. To steal Bitcoin, a hacker would have to alter the ledger on every computer on the network.

To destroy a bitcoin account, would be to destroy every computer on the planet that hosts a bitcoin account.

Even if by some miracle someone could ever hack an account, it would not be worth the effort. If it were hacked, Bitcoin would no longer be trusted as money and as such will become worthless, leaving the stolen Bitcoin worthless.

Quantity of Bitcoin

Each bitcoin is divisible up to 100,000 'Satoshis'. Satoshi Nakamoto being the name of the anonymous person or persons who created Bitcoin.

The reward for mining bitcoin was originally 50 bitcoins per block. This reward is halved every four years and currently stands at 12.5 bitcoins per block.

The maximum amount of bitcoin that can ever be mined is 21 million. This amount is forecast to be reached in the year 2140.

The flow of bitcoin into the network is controlled by:

• Adjusting the difficulty of the maths problem within the hash algorithm.
• Reducing the bitcoin reward every four years.

Combined, these mechanisms ensure that flow of bitcoin will not be disproportionate to stock.

Is Bitcoin good money?

We learned in Skill 6 that real money must meet these criteria:

- Medium of exchange and unit of account
- Portable
- Durable
- Divisible
- Fungible (Interchangeable)
- A store of value

How does Bitcoin do against these:

Medium of exchange.

Portability: Excellent – It's always in your pocket in any quantity.

Durability: Excellent – Could only be affected by an internet shutdown.

Divisibility: Excellent - Each Bitcoin is 100,000 Satoshis.

Fungability: Excellent. Every unit is interchangeable.

A store of value. Excellent.

A store of value

You can understand why many investors see cryptocurrency as a good bet: it meets all the criteria of real money in the same way as gold and silver.

It also has another quality that makes it really good and this is its 'stock to flow ratio'.

As we have seen in Skill 11, the notes and coins and commercial bank currency in use today can be devalued very quickly by central banks typing more currency into existence, or by banks lending money. Hence our currency is not a store of value. Gold has kept its store of value primarily because the supply is limited. Gold is difficult and costly to mine, and it's scarce. When gold prices are low, mining companies shut down their operations and mine other more attractively priced commodities.

This scarcity means the stock to flow ratio is always low and cannot be manipulated like our currency is today.

This principle is the same for Bitcoin. The stock is controlled by the minors and a new coin is produced every ten minutes, until in 2041 when the maximum 21 million will be mined.

Bitcoin cannot be manipulated and has a finite supply, therefore there is no inflation and it is truly a store of value.

The future of Crypto

While decentralisation renders Bitcoin government-free, and that is a massive attraction for investors; there is also no governing authority to assist if it goes wrong. Although it is difficult to think of what could go wrong, setting aside the internet crashing.

Crypto, unlike gold that can be used to make jewellery, has no intrinsic value. It is only worth what people think it is worth.

Some governments have already frozen Bitcoin accounts and issued subpoenas to Bitcoin holders, demanding they divulge information about their accounts. And that is the problem with crypto for me. Just like in 1933, when Franklin D. Roosevelt confiscated the gold and silver of the American people, so too could crypto be legislated against. For this reason, I'd not hold crypto personally.

Are they a good investment?

Possibly, but only as a speculative investment in my opinion. With no intrinsic value and open to the whims of government, it is worth what the market agrees it's worth. As a result, crypto has shown to be very volatile and its future is very unclear.

With the added risk of a possible new government 'digital system of exchange' and potential risk of restrictions, as well as the advent of quantum computers which could at some stage crack encryption codes, it's not an investment class I'd get involved with.

But I'm sure there are many out there such as Simon Dixon and Ashton Kutcher, who have been involved with Bitcoin from the near beginning, who would disagree.

SKILL 23: INVESTING IN LAND

Now we are back to the tangible investments that I like. For the record, there is not one wealthy person I know who doesn't own land; the rich certainly prioritise it as an investment and always have. Bill Gates is buying-up half of America it seems.

We bought some woodland recently so that the family and our staff could use it for camping trips. Woodland sites have increased in value by over 50% in the last five years I was surprised to learn, so they are great investments and small sites can be picked up relatively inexpensively.

Although land in general is and always has been a great investment, it is like gold in some ways, in that it seems to have performed as a store of value over the years and from time to time, like at present, well outperforms inflation. But like gold will not give you a cash flow.

But why would you buy land over say gold and other investments?

We bought ours for two reasons. We had spare cash and wanted to put it into an appreciating asset, as we did not want to leave it in the bank where it will depreciate. Also, we wanted to use the land for our enjoyment, so it was a win-win.

House builders buy land speculatively, hoping one day to obtain planning permission. They sometimes hold on to land for many years, steadily plugging away at the planners in the hope that the planning laws in that area will lighten up, as they often do, and they will be granted planning permission.

Generally speaking, the more likelihood of obtaining planning permission on a piece of land, the more expensive it will be. Land with planning consent is very expensive.

We currently have a small piece of land we paid £40,000 for six years ago. We have just sold it for £165,000 because we have a letter from the planning authority saying they would support an application on the piece of land. £125,000 profit for virtually no work. This is the sort of money that can be made on land deals.

This is the reason developers buy land, there is some good money to be made.

There are many companies that specialise in buying and selling land. They use architects and planning consultants to badger the planning authority and when they eventually do obtain consent, sell-on the land to investors, builders and developers at a considerable profit.

We have just bought two acres of land for £600,000 that used to be someone's back garden. We intend to build a big house on the site. When we checked back how much the investor paid for the site four years earlier, he'd paid £700,000 for our plot and the adjacent plot. The person who bought the adjacent plot paid £700,000. That's a profit for the investor of £600,000 in four years and all they had to do was obtain planning consent.

It took six months to complete on the purchase and a few days after, we were offered £700,000. It had increased in value by £100,000.

How do you find land?

There are many land brokers; companies that specialise in finding land and you can sign-up to their mailing list. The properties they tend to have are expensive. They have already taken a lump of the margin out of the site, making it difficult for the average investor or developer to make a good margin. But this is only my experience.

It's easy to find land on a Google Earth search of properties with large back gardens. Many investors use this strategy. Then start a conversation with the owner to sell off some of their garden and work out a mutually beneficial deal. This is an excellent strategy.

Another good strategy is just driving around looking for old houses with big gardens. Then buying them with a view to putting a larger house or multiple houses on the site. This is a great way to make a lot of money quickly.

Google Earth is a great tool for that and you can focus in on the area you want. This strategy is absolutely a win-win. The home owner benefits from selling their garden and the investor can sell-on the plot at a nice margin.

Along with houses, we very much intend to make land a part of our investment strategy moving forward.

SKILL 24:
BUILDING A BUSINESS
AS AN INVESTMENT

No doubt some of you will be wanting to start your own business at some stage. This Skill is for you.

You may be wondering why I've put building a business in the Investment section. Because building a business can be an amazing investment strategy. It can be an excellent way to get lumps of cash to invest in other assets in a very tax efficient way and give you a steady cash-flow.

The investment strategies so far can all be done part-time, but running a business is something most have to devote their life to. Also, other strategies can be learned relatively quickly, while building a business requires a great deal of knowledge.

If you intend to start a business, and I'd urge you to do so, you need to educate yourself in all the core business skills before you start. I've found people often dive in the deep-end, driven by passion, and fail in their first year as most businesses do.

One of the major mistakes people make is not understanding business finances. Knowledge of how to read a Profit and Loss Account, P&L, Balance Sheet and Management Accounts is essential for anyone thinking of going into business. You can't just leave this to the accountant, you need to keep on-top of your finances daily.

The business-investment model

My sons and I use our family building business as a cash-cow for our investments. We plough most of the profits into property, building solid appreciating assets and passive income, which will be a legacy for future generations.

It's an excellent model because when the business is profitable chunks of cash can be used to buy cash-flowing assets, which will mean you will become financially free much quicker than you would have been by working for someone else for a wage.

Tax

One big reason for investing through a business is tax savings.

If you are an employee, all your savings have been taxed. The government take a big lump of your hard-earned money and it will take you longer to save up a deposit for your rental property.

If you have a business you can just use profits to buy houses gross, no tax. If you are a higher rate taxpayer the saving could be over 50% if you include National Insurance.

But you need a profitable business to start with and building a business is no easy option and is certainly not for everyone.

If you do have aspirations of running your own business, let me share some of my experience with you here.

What it takes to build a business

I would urge anyone to start their own business – it can give you more freedom and more money, eventually.

But we have to be realistic: over half of new businesses fail. They fail for many different reasons, but in reality, it all comes down to one thing: lack of the appropriate business skills. Having been a business owner now for over 36 years, I feel qualified to give you an insider's view of the type of skills you will need. These are as follows:

Accepting responsibility

I hope you can take on responsibility? It's a biggie. Perhaps the most important trait of the entrepreneur is the ability to take on large amounts of responsibility. I tell the story in my first book (50 Skills – The Entrepreneurs' Handbook) of an experienced site manager who called the office several times a day to ask menial things like, "where should I place the signs"; he took every opportunity to pass off the responsibility to someone else.

Most people are not built to take on much responsibility nor do they want to. It plays on their mind, stops them from sleeping and leads to anxiety. If this is you, business may not be for you.

Self-confidence

As a business owner, as your business grows, you will be called upon to do all sorts of things that the average person would shy away from, including taking risks, chairing meetings, client meetings, interviewing new staff and of course the dreaded public speaking.

A recent article said that some people would rather die than do public speaking. I don't know about that, but I know it can be daunting. But it's a skill you'll need to learn and a fear to conquer if you want to run a business. The first big presentation I did, I froze. This is definitely a learned skill.

Self-belief

Can you trust yourself over all others? There are occasions in business when all around you will be doubting your opinion. If you really feel your way is the right way, sometimes you have to have enough belief in your idea to push on and make it work, in spite of the naysayers. Accepting responsibility for your actions right or wrong.

It takes a lot for a person to go against the crowd, peer pressure can be an immense emotion, as the recent wearing of masks has shown, but one the entrepreneur must manage.

Think way ahead

Its no-good living in the day if you are an entrepreneur. Strategic thinking is another vital skill. Most people only think a few days ahead, but as a business owner you need to think years ahead, even decades.

You need the ability to envision the future by building a strong image in your mind. Then develop new systems to cope with your future vision. You need the ability to get others to buy-in to your vision; that's where persuasion skills and public speaking come in.

Day-to-day thinking is for operational staff, future thinking is the job of the entrepreneur. Can you think ahead? Our family are planning a generation ahead.

Delegation

Do you say things like, "I'll do it myself, that way I know it'll get done properly"? I hope not, because you could struggle to delegate and lack trust in others.

There are always people who can do the job better than you; in fact, that's just the type of person you want to employ. It will free you up and allow you as the strategist to think ahead and take a helicopter view of the business, keeping out of the day-to-day. But it takes courage to let go of the important stuff – that's why so many business owners can't grow their businesses, they stay small enough that they personally can keep control.

Be great at systems

This again is a learned skill which I personally love. Think McDonald's, a well-oiled machine.

As you grow you'll need to systemise the business. Think of systems like the skeleton of the business, they provide a framework so everyone knows who does what and what goes where. They create order out of chaos.

Systemising means breaking down tasks into a series of logical stages, removing any overlaps or duplications. Entrepreneurs need this skill which can be learned. The E-Myth, by Michael E Gerber, would be a good place for you to start to learn how to write systems, a must read for any business owner. My first book also has a big section on writing systems.

Be a great teacher

Can you pass on your skills? Once you have written the systems, you will need to put your idea across to others in a logical way. Poor implementation of a new idea is where most people go wrong and systems fall down.

Implementing a new system means change, and people resist change. You will need to be persistent, good at preparing and carrying out presentations and have good powers of persuasion. Getting staff buy-in by letting them help you put the system together will help a lot.

Handle stress

I would say it is possible for most people to learn how to handle stress. But for others stress can be devastating, leading to ill health if not dealt with.

As a business owner, you must be able to handle large amounts of stress and not let it affect your sleep and your health. Most people cannot.

There are amazing techniques for dealing with stress and anxiety and the best book I've read on the subject is Overcoming Anxiety by Helen Kennerley, a must read.

Self-discipline

Can you say no to the chocolate in the fridge? I can't either. All jokes aside, you must be self-motivated and self-disciplined in business. Sometimes sacrifices have to be made, like staying late at work or missing the gym, working weekends and missing football or giving up your time to study. You'll sometimes get pressure from the family too, and have to find ways to compromise and keep the business and the family happy.

Determination

There will be times when you need to prioritise what you are doing at work over other areas in your life, perhaps because of some deadline or emergency. You need to be the sort of person to step-up a gear, dig-in and get the job done; nothing must get in your way.

At such times, you need to stay determined and prioritise this over all else. This could mean in the short-term giving up hobbies or a social life. Many people don't want to make such sacrifices, but it's all part of being a business owner.

Persuasive skills

This is a very important skill. As leader and strategist, you will know where you want to take the business. This is all well and good, but in most cases change means directly affecting someone's working practices or life. You have to present your idea in such a way that it will be appealing to your team and have something in it for everyone. That can be difficult. Persuasion is beyond the scope of this book but covered in some detail in my first book.

Empathy

You've either got it or you haven't. My son Adam bought ice lollies for the entire office one day but was one short, so Adam gave his lolly to the person in accounts who took the lolly. The event was overheard by my son Alex, who a short while later went out without saying a word and returned with a lolly for Adam. That's an example of empathy. People with empathy rise to the top like cream. Why? Because his action met an important law of the universe. The law of, 'you give me a sweetie and I'll give you a bag of sweeties'. Ok it's not a real law of the universe, but a law I live by. It means if you do something for someone without their asking (or even with), most people will do something even greater for you.

As MD, you are there for one thing: to serve your staff. It is they who will make you rich. You need to think of yourself as a father figure and be there for your team when they need you. This cannot be an act. It has to be genuine from the heart or you will soon get found out.

I've found that people are motivated by recognition from their boss. In practice, this means giving your time for a chat, a coffee, having an open-door policy. Selfish bosses find that staff rarely stay around too long. If you are not the sort of person to have empathy or make time for others, you'll struggle to keep staff.

Do what you say you are going to do

I do feel this is another inherent trait. Bull-shitters, as my dad and now I call them, never last long in business. Or if they do, rarely grow their business. They just go from one client to another after they get found out for what they are.

I am sad to say my experience has been that at least half the senior people I've employed fall into this category. Many haven't the balls to be straight with you. They'd rather tell little white lies than face up to a difficult conversation. But you'll need to if you intend to build a business; straight talking and honesty is the only way.

Drive to succeed

My driving force now comes from two main sources. First, my drive to see my sons and grandchildren have amazing lives, and second, my drive to keep my current financially-free lifestyle.

Having a strong driving force has helped me do extraordinary things outside of my comfort zone. Like doing big presentations to staff and clients, or go knock on a client's office who hasn't paid us, or cold call when we were short of work, re-mortgage my house to put money into the business to cover a short-term cash-flow issue, and much more. Necessity is a great motivator.

Are you a rule breaker?

You need to be. I'm not suggesting you go out and break rules for the sake of it; especially those aimed at safety in society, like speeding on the road. Nor am I suggesting you break the rules to cheat in business; that would be wrong too.

But, many rules are made by people for their own interests, or they are just plain stupid rules. What I am suggesting is that you should not comply with silly rules or rules made by people who do not have your interests at heart.

Instead you should take a good look at the rule and assess this from a common-sense perspective and ask, 'does this rule serve any good purpose to people? Is it fair? Is it sensible?'. If the answer is no, then find an alternative solution.

I find that most of the general public follow the rules, many to the letter. Rarely do they think for themselves and ask why they are following silly rules and rarely do these people last long in business. In business and in life, question everything and come to your own conclusion. In the words of the great Steve Jobs and now me, "everything you have ever known has been designed for you by someone else". I would add, "who doesn't have your interest at heart".

My mantra is, does what I am about to do harm or bring injustice to my 'fellow man'. If not, do it.

Do you think large corporations or governments follow rules? Most definitely not. Moreover, large corporations like the tech giants, big pharma and big oil put millions into lobbying and manipulating governments and other global entities like the World Health Organization to change the rules to suit their own needs. Have you noticed how Amazon have thrived during the lockdown? Funny how they were allowed to stay open while all the highstreets shops had to close. How many small businesses have gone under while Amazon makes billions due to bad rules serving a minority interest?

On a side note, the media are complicit in this. They reinforce the big corporations and the government's bad rules through television propaganda. But that's a rabbit hole for another book.

Rules are for guidance only, they are not the law. Common law says do no harm to your 'fellow man', anything else is a statute which often suits the interests of a few over the interests of the many. So be careful which rules you follow.

In business, you need to have a questioning and determined mind-set not to abide by rules that are against your interests. Be a rule breaker.

Business skills

You notice that many of the above were personality traits, the soft skills. Along with this you will need a great deal of hard business skills which can all be learned, but not in college. Learned by reading appropriate books and from mentors who have been there and done it.

By hard business skills I mean things like accounting and finance skills, dealing with banks, managing staff, business structures, sales and marketing, and business development.

Good mentors are hard to come by as they are usually still building businesses, they tend to be doers rather than teachers. If you find one that has built a successful business they will be very expensive, but well worth it.

Still thinking of starting a business? I hope so.

If you are still thinking that building a business sounds like something you feel comfortable with, then game-on, business could be for you. But if in your heart you know that some of the things I've discussed just aren't you, have a good think before you make the leap into business. You can still make it by being an employee, just be a good one and get paid as much as you can.

If you have read the above and you are filled with excitement at the thought of the freedom and money a business can bring, you may want to read my book, 50 Skills – The Entrepreneurs' Handbook, where I break business down into bite-sized, understandable chunks and discuss the soft and the hard skills you will need to start and grow a business. I also provide a step-by-step template to plan your new business.

BONUS SECTION: MONEY ESSENTIALS FOR LIFE

In the bonus section I cover the subjects below which did not readily fit into any other category discussed so far, but are still relevant to your financial future.

I've gone into some detail on each category, giving you some insider tips to prepare you for dealing with the various sales people on these transactions so you can get the best result.

The information could save you a lot of money and wasted time, as I found out learning the hard way.

None of this was taught to me at school and as the great psychologist Jordan Peterson said, "they bloody-well should have".

25. Opening A Bank Account
26. Buying a Car
27. Renting a Property
28. Getting a Mortgage
29. Obtain Loans & Credit Scores
30. Organising your Finances

SKILL 25: OPENING A BANK ACCOUNT

Its 100% certain that you are going need a bank account if you don't already have one. But even if you do, here are some tips which may help you in the future.

A DuckDuckGo search or the bank's own website will lead you through the steps required to open a bank account and it's a lengthy process that will differ from bank to bank.

My purpose here is to tell you what the banks do not tell you, so you know what to look-out for before you open an account. Then you can choose the best account and bank for you.

The first question to ask yourself is, who do I open my account with? This can be confusing as there are over 300 banks and 45 building societies in the UK. But there are generally considered to be four main high street banks. These are Barclays, Lloyds, HSBC and NatWest in order of size.

Most of us need a current account for day-to-day transactions, and a savings account, so convenience could be the major consideration when choosing a bank. If this is the case then the larger banks are more likely to have not only a greater range of products including Apps, but also more branches and automated teller machines, commonly known as ATMs or Cash machines. If convenience is what you are after, one of the big four would probably fit the bill.

Another reason to choose a big bank is that they are backed by the government, meaning the government would not let them fail, as we learned can happen in Skill 11.

I remember my first experience of opening an account at age 16 when my first employer took me to the local NatWest. All I needed was my personal information and in a matter of days the account was open.

It's a little more complicated now. All transactions of a financial nature, not just opening a bank account, require a person to provide identification under the Proceeds of Crime Act to prevent money laundering (money derived from an illegal source). You will need identification – a passport, birth certificate, driving licence or adoption certificate – and proof of your address or a letter from your university or college confirming your place, dated within the last three months. You will need to produce these when you go to open the account. If you apply online, the bank will need to see the originals.

Open Two Accounts

You should consider opening accounts with two banks. Get settled in one, then open another. This is important for several reasons. First, you are building relationships with two banks and if you fall out with one you have the other. You can also use your second account as leverage. For example, my bank once charged me for going into overdraft for one day. I argued the point but they refused to refund me. When I said I had a longstanding relationship with a competitor of theirs and would take all my business there, they refunded the money.

It also increases your chances of obtaining a bank loan or even a mortgage later on and is just good practice. You could, for example, use one as your current account and one for savings.

Direct debts and standing orders

No doubt over time you will have to pay a person or organisation regular amounts of money from your bank. Direct Debits or Standing Orders can be set-up with your bank to allow payments to come out at regular intervals. DDs and SOs are very good ways to organise your finances and give you peace of mind that you have not missed a payment.

A Direct Debit is when you authorise an organisation to collect money directly from your bank account whenever a payment is due. These may be monthly car premiums, council tax, utility bills etc.

A Standing Order is an instruction you give to your bank to pay a fixed amount at regular intervals to another bank, whether this is weekly, monthly, quarterly or yearly. This could be to another person for paying back say a personal loan, rent or other regular payment.

It is a very good idea to organise your finances and set-up DDs or SOs, which is very easy to do online and through the banking App on your phone.

One note of caution. If you cancel a DD early without notifying the company, this could negatively affect your credit score and you certainly do not want that as we shall see in Skill 29.

Debit and credit cards

Debit Card

The Debit Card whether physical or mobile App is linked to your current account. When you pay for anything on a Debit Card the money is taken immediately from your account, so you'd better make sure funds are available, or have an agreed overdraft to cover the amount. Debit cards are used mainly to pay for day-to-day goods and to withdraw money at cash machines.

Credit Card

There are over 60 Credit Card providers online, 15 of whom are based in the UK. All will offer different rates and deals at different times.

The Credit Card, be it physical or by Mobile App, is independent of your bank account. A credit card enables you to buy things up to a pre-arranged limit, and pay for them at a later date. The cost of the purchase is added to your credit card account and you get a statement every month.

You then have a choice of paying off the bill in full by a set date with no interest, or paying at least a minimum amount and spreading the repayments over a period of time, in which case you will pay interest on the balance.

I don't own a credit card and I would prefer that you didn't either, as it's very easy to get into debt as the interest can be very high. That said, it is a good idea to use a Credit Card at least in the early days, as this will help improve your credit score, providing you make regular payments.

Again, a note of caution. If you have a change of address, please notify the credit card company, or anyone you owe money to for that matter. If a payment gets missed even for no fault of your own, this could affect your credit score. As I found out to my detriment.

Overdraft facility

This is an amount of money the bank has agreed to offer you after your bank account is empty. Of course, the bank will charge you interest when you are in overdraft and a yearly charge for having the facility.

Your chances of getting an overdraft depends on your risk profile with the bank. A good time to ask for an overdraft is when you open the account as you have more leverage. Banks love young people, they look at them as an investment in their future. You may not be earning much or borrowing much now, but as you get older you probably will.

Banks try all sorts of marketing ploys to entice young people, with add-ons like free overdraft facilities, free fees for the first year etc. In the hope they will have you as a customer forever, and can recoup their investment many times over.

All banks offer different incentives and it is a good idea to shop around to get the best deal for you.

SKILL 26: BUYING A CAR

....

One of the nicer things in life is to go car hunting, especially if it's your first car. But it can also be stressful, because you are about to sign-up to a big financial commitment. So here are some tips from a person who considers himself an expert car buyer, having bought a lot of cars in his time and made a lot of mistakes.

First you will need a provisional licence. You can apply for one at age 15 years and nine months at the time of writing. This allows you to drive a moped or light quad bike. Then you'll have to wait until you are 17 to take your theory test for which you will need the provisional licence. Assuming you pass your theory test and then your driving test, you are good-to-go to buy a car.

Buy with your head not your heart

My first piece of advice, which you will undoubtedly not take, is to buy the car with the head and not your heart. Car salespeople are expert at getting you to buy from the heart, which always costs you more. The car you should buy, the less expensive standard model, leaves you feeling a bit flat. But the GT version with the alloy wheels and flash paint job gets you excited just looking at it. You imagine what your mates will say, how jealous they will be. I'll be honest, the heart usually wins over the head when buying a car and the salespeople know it.

I'm probably not the best person to give you this advice – or maybe I am, I've been rubbish at resisting expensive cars over the years, much to the detriment of my bank account. But if I could turn back the clock, I'd have definitely bought houses that made me money rather than cars that cost me money. That way I could have let the rental income pay for the cars.

Buying options

Assuming you've taken my advice and found a nice inexpensive car, you now have several buying options.

I remember in my early days of car buying, the salesperson explaining to me the various options available for me to buy the car. I could see his lips move, but my head was hearing blah, blah, blah. Then when he asked me how I'd like to finance the car at the end of his spiel, I just stared at him with a blank look on my face.

All this can get very confusing, so let me break it down for you here.

- Personal Contract Purchase PCP
- Hire Purchase HP
- Leasing
- Bank loan
- Cash

Personal Contract Purchase PCP

This is a good option if you like changing your car every two or three years and a common method that most dealerships will offer you.

You will need to put down a deposit – the minimum is 1% of the cost of the car but more usually 10%. A finance company will then pay the balance for you to the dealer and you will pay the finance company a regular monthly payment for a period of time. This could be two, three or four years whichever suits you, but obviously the less the period the more the monthly payments.

The monthly payments are calculated to pay off two-thirds of the cost. At the end of the term you have what is called a balloon payment, which is the final third of the cost.

You then have choices.

- Return the car to the dealer and hand back the keys.
- Pay off the balloon payment and the car is yours.
- Use the car as a deposit for a new car and the process is repeated.

The first two options are fairly straightforward, although there may be on-costs if you have damaged the car or gone over the agreed mileage. But you do need to be careful with the last option.

When you originally bought the car, the salesperson would have told you that there will be equity left in the car. In other words, the car will be worth more than you owe and that you can use this as the deposit on a new vehicle. I am very reliably informed by a good friend who is in the industry that there rarely, if ever, is any equity, unless you put a big deposit down in the first place.

It is a good idea to do your research into the possible resale value of your vehicle at the end of the term. Do not take the dealer's word for it.

Hire purchase – HP

Another common method of purchase is the HP agreement. This works in a similar way to a mortgage, in that you will put in a deposit then pay the balance in instalments over an agreed term. Usually one to five years.

The payments will be capital and interest which means that each payment is made up of part of the loan plus interest, calculated as follows:

The car loan divided by the term of the agreement in months, plus the agreed interest.

At the end of the period, the car is yours.

This is my preferred method to buy a vehicle as it is owned outright at the end of the term. There are also no mileage restrictions which is a bonus.

Leasing

There are several types of lease arrangement and some can be confusing. People often get caught out when leasing and get fleeced at the end of the term because they didn't fully understand what they were signing up to. It is very important to know at the outset what are signing up-to at the end.

There are three options for leasing you should know about:

- Personal Contract Purchase (Discussed Above)
- Personal Contract Hire
- Personal Lease Purchase

Personal Contract Hire

This is by far the preferred method. You simply rent the car for an agreed term and hand back at the end.

This is like renting a flat in that you pay a fixed monthly fee over an agreed period of time, usually two to four years. You will need to put in a deposit which could be up to six times the monthly payment.

At the outset, you and the dealer will agree the annual mileage you require, then, when the car is returned the mileage will be checked. The driver will have to pay for any additional miles at a rate agreed in the contract which can be from 4p up to 70p per mile. So, it's a good idea to allow more than enough miles per year at the outset.

At the end of the period the agreed mileage and condition of the car will be assessed and you will be charged for excess mileage or damage. But if you are under the mileage with fair wear and tear on the vehicle, you can hand it back with no further implication.

Regarding fair wear and tear to the vehicle, in my experience they are ruthless in their assessment of fair wear and tear, and you will often have to negotiate hard if you think they have overcharged you.

Personal Lease Purchase

If you want a new car but cannot afford expensive monthly payments, then a Personal Lease Purchase deal could be for you. Like all other purchase options you will have to put in an initial deposit then monthly payments over two – four years.

At the end of the term you will have to pay a 'balloon payment' and the car will then be yours.

Bank loan

Another way to raise money for a car is by bank loan. Then you have the money to go pay cash for your new car. There are a few good reasons for doing this.

You may get a better interest rate with the bank. You could get a bank loan today for say 4%. You will pay around 6% through a finance company. You may even get more time to pay back the loan back, five years in some cases. This will reduce your monthly payments.

SKILL 26: BUYING A CAR

The other advantage is that your bank will love you. As we know, there is nothing more a bank likes than to lend you money at interest. It's why they exist. Don't ever think banks won't like you if you borrow money; they won't like you if you don't.

There are a few things you need to consider if you do choose this route. If you crash the car and write it off (make it economically unviable to repair), you still owe the bank all the money. The right insurance cover becomes very important and you may even consider GAP insurance, which guarantees a pay-out of the original purchase price should the car get written-off.

The other good reason to get a bank loan is that you will own the car at the end of the term.

Cash

You may think as I did, that as a cash buyer you have good bargaining power. This is not the case these days; dealers make more money if you use finance, as they get commission from the finance company.

It may still be beneficial to use cash to negotiate in some small second-hand car dealers. But nowadays the industry is more sophisticated and cash is no longer king.

Point of sale add-ons

The car industry has become very creative in the ways it can push up margin and squeeze money out of you. Car dealers make their money in several ways, not just the sale of the car.

Firstly, they add a mark-up to the manufacturer's price and this differs depending on market conditions. Also, if you finance the vehicle the dealer gets a cut from the finance company. Then there are a series of what are known as add-ons. This is where the dealers will try to up-sell you right at the point-of-sale, when you are all fired-up and excited about your new car, and most vulnerable. Dealers are becoming more and more creative with upselling add-ons. Here are the usual suspects you could be offered:

- Gap insurance
- Alloy wheel damage cover
- Paint protection
- Dent cover
- Car service plans

The dealer makes money on all these and will try to persuade you to buy, saying things like, "most people buy this" or "you really need this".

Whether you buy or not is up to you. I don't buy any of them, apart from the service plans that can sometimes save you money.

Negotiation

As I said previously, in my younger day I stupidly bought lots of cars and over the years I got quite good at negotiating a good deal. So here are some tips.

The first thing to remember is that you never pay the asking price, always go in with the attitude that you are going to get a deal.

The second thing to remember is that you are dealing with trained salespeople. They will likely have sat in a room with someone giving them sales techniques to help them sell you a more expensive car than you wanted to buy. Do not underestimate the skill of some of these people – they can be very subtle and persuasive and even the more experienced and hardened negotiators like me get caught out. So be strong and buy with your head.

My advice is take someone with you who isn't emotionally attached, who has your best interests at heart.

When you go car hunting, be prepared for a long day. You could be in the car showroom for hours with nothing but the coffee machine, so take some refreshments with you.

The process is a long one, from walking around looking at cars, then walking around again with the salesperson showing you the benefits of the car. Then sitting down with the salesperson, taking personal details, deciding if it's a PCP or HP, how many years you want the deal over; different deal options can all take hours. Be prepared for a lot of friendly small talk as well, it's all part of the sales process, but don't get taken in.

The salesperson will *always* try to get out of you the maximum amount you would like to pay monthly, always. Never ever tell the truth. Because, trust me when I say that whatever you say, the deal will miraculously be just a little more than that figure, always. If you said £200, it will work out at £232. It's always an odd figure too, as if they have spent ages working it out. If you have £200 in your mind, say £150. If the dealer can't make that price, ask for his best price. Turn the tables on them.

Let's assume the dealer tells you the monthly payment is £232. Now you must negotiate. Never accept that offer. Go back with a counter offer – "could you do that for £190?".

What happens during the negotiation is slightly weird. The sales person disappears for ten minutes or more saying, "let me discuss your offer with my manager". Then comes back and says, "I've spoken to the boss and we can't do that. But we can do it for £230 and give you the alloy wheel protection thrown in, which normally retails at £500."

I hope you are getting the picture – there will be a lot of toing and froing, but you must bargain hard and be patient.

In most instances, you will get some sort of discount, but occasionally, when there is a big market for the car, the price will be the price. They just don't care if you don't buy the car, another punter will be through the door as soon as you walk out.

One more interesting note. Always go car hunting near the end of the month. Car dealerships work their figures and bonuses monthly. You will get more of a discount near the end of the month as they need the sale for the month-end figures to ensure bonuses. Doing a deal on say the 27th of the month is good as long as the deal can be completed on or before the last day of the month.

New or used

Do you buy new or do you buy used? This is the question.

Used car dealers can offer similar finance products to main dealers on new cars, so unless you are paying cash, it's really down to the monthly payment. Zero percent finance is usually only available on new car sales.

I always buy new or almost new cars and own them for two-three years. That way I am sure the car will be safe and will start first time every time. If you buy second hand you have no way of knowing what has happened to the car and its reliability. Generally speaking, the older the car, the less reliable and the more you will spend on servicing and repairs, not to mention the inconvenience and time wasted.

You could buy a car for say £1500 cash or even less, but will it start every time? Who knows. If you're a car mechanic, no problem, but if you are the average Joe who relies on his car for work, constant breakdowns could be a real hassle.

Whether you pay cash or buy a car through finance is really down to your personal choice and circumstances. For me, I'd go with a regular monthly payment, so I can organise my finances around that.

Happy car hunting.

SKILL 27: RENTING A PROPERTY

....

This Skill has been written by my very talented youngest son, Alex, aged 19. Alex runs our property side and can deal with these topics better than I can. Over to Alex.

At some stage in life you may want to rent a property or rent out your own property for that matter. The following information will help in both regards.

This skill is broken up into the sections shown:

- Finding a property to rent
- Referencing & Credit checks
- Type of tenancy

Finding a property to rent

As a tenant, you can rent a property directly with a landlord if you can find one, or more commonly through a letting agent.

The best way to source a property is online using property portals such as Rightmove and Zoopla. Most properties on the rental market are added to these sites and they allow you to get in touch with the person or company letting the property to show your interest and arrange a viewing.

Another way to find a property is to call letting agents in the area. This is a good idea because there are sometimes properties that haven't been put onto Rightmove yet, known as 'off-market properties', which may be perfect for you.

There are a number of questions you should ask before deciding to rent a particular property. These are as follows:

What is the council Tax band for the property?

Properties in the UK are banded from A-D. Bands are decided from the property's value in 1991, higher value properties are assigned to a higher band. As you can imagine with properties built after 1991, this banding can be slightly misjudged in some cases.

You are able to challenge a council tax band if you feel your property has been judged incorrectly. You do this by contacting the valuation office agency.

Does the landlord allow pets?

If you have pets you may not be able to apply for some properties. It is always worth asking the question as there may be exceptions in certain situations, especially if the landlord is having difficulty renting the property. So even if it says no pets on the advert, ask anyway.

Dogs are often the most common type of pet which is not allowed. Sometimes smaller dogs which are less likely to cause damage are allowed by the landlord. Often cats are allowed as well. The main thing to remember is to always ask the question just in case. In some cases, the landlord may apply an extra charge for pets in case of damage.

Is the property furnished?

Properties are available fully furnished down to cutlery and towels in the bathroom. Or part furnished with only the main items of furniture included. Or completely unfurnished. Furnished properties are obviously more expensive than un-furnished.

Landlords are often very accommodating to tenants' requirements, and if you are a good prospective tenant but require furniture, often a deal can be struck, so please ask the question.

Are bills included?

This is a key piece of information when making a decision to rent a property. Some properties are available with the rental payment covering the council tax, electric, gas and water bills. This will be reflected in a higher rent.

Sometimes not all bills are included. This is most commonly council tax. You should definitely check this, so you don't get a nasty surprise.

Transport links and local amenities

It's very important to ensure the property is situated in a convenient area for your work and social life (hopefully you will get one back soon), and that there are convenient transport links.

Referencing & credit checks

It is best to be open and honest when applying for a property, regarding your situation, especially your financial situation. Checks will be carried out based on the information you have provided. If the information is not accurate, it will be found out during the checking process and will lead to you losing the property.

Even if you have had issues in the past, flag them up and be honest; this will build trust.

Before renting a property, you are going to be asked for a series of documents to undergo a referencing and credit check process. The more prepared you are for this the better, as it will make the process quicker and easier.

Ensure you have the following in preparation:

- 3 months' pay slips
- Reference from employer
- Reference from current landlord
- Passport / Driving Licence
- If self-employed – 2 years' SA302s – tax return
- If self-employed – 6 months' bank statements – Business and personal

If you are not employed but self-employed and have been operating for under 12 months, most of the time you will be asked for a guarantor for the rent. Meaning, should you not pay your rent (default), this person would be contractually obligated to pay on your behalf.

A guarantor is usually a parent, but can be anyone. Ensure that it is a person you trust. The guarantor will usually be referenced and credit checked in the same way that you are.

To be successful, a monthly income of at least 2.5 times the monthly rent is required. Make sure you are in a position to afford the rent.

You will need identification (ID) in order for the 'Right to Rent' check to be carried out. This is to ensure that you are a citizen of the UK or EEA.

Your credit score (Skill 29) is of utmost importance during this process. Ensure that you look at your credit report before applying for a rental property. Remember that all credit agencies are legally obliged to provide you with one free report per year, if you ask.

In the credit check, County Court Judgements, CCJs, or Individual Voluntary Arrangements, IVAs, will be picked up if you have any. Often this could lead to you being unsuccessful in applying for the property, so be sure to inform the agent/landlord of any marks against your credit score at the earliest point. If you highlight this early enough in the process you may be more likely to be accepted, as trust is established.

A CCJ is a mark against your credit score given when you have missed a payment for a prolonged period of time. This is applied for, by the entity you have missed the payment with, through the court.

An IVA is a payment plan set up to pay off any debts such as CCJs.

You will usually be asked to fill out an application form to provide information on yourself at the start of the process.

Under the 'Tenant Fee Act 2019' you are not allowed to be charged any fees for referencing and credit checks. The only thing you can be charged for is one week's rent holding deposit. This is explained further below.

A final note on the referencing process. Be cautious when a landlord or agent does not bother carrying out checks on you. This may seem good at first, but can highlight that they follow a bad practice and may be difficult to deal with later on in the tenancy. This is not always the case, but good to keep in mind.

Deposit

There are two types of deposit you may come across when renting a property, a Holding Deposit and a Security Deposit.

Holding Deposit

Some landlords and letting agencies will charge a holding deposit prior to referencing and credit checks. This is because it costs them money to do the checks and they want you to commit. Once paid, the property would be reserved for you subject to successful completion of references. The maximum amount of holding deposit is equivalent to one week's rent, or monthly rental amount divided by 4.33.

The holding deposit cannot be charged as a fee for referencing. If you pass through the checks successfully, the holding deposit should be returned to you. In our letting agency, we include the amount in the first month's rent.

There are two times which the landlord/agent can retain the holding deposit:

- If after referencing and credit checks it is found you submitted false information at the application stage leading to the rejection of your application.
- If you decide to back out of an application.

Security Deposit

This is a sum of money held by the landlord as insurance against you damaging the property during the course of the tenancy.

At the start of the tenancy a condition survey is carried out and documented. At the end of the tenancy, the condition of the property is compared to the survey and any damage noted. An agreement is made between the landlord and tenant as to the amount of deposit to be retained by the landlord, the excess being returned to the tenant.

The condition of the property from the start to the end of the tenancy is called the inventory. The report carried out at the end is called the checkout report.

It is important that you receive a copy of both reports. This is because if the landlord decides to deduct an amount from your security deposit which you feel is unfair, you can use the reports as proof.

When a landlord holds a security deposit it has to be paid into a government scheme, or retained by the landlord and the amount insured by the government scheme.

At the end of the tenancy, if an agreement cannot be made on the deposit return amount, the case is handed to an independent adjudicator who decides the amount for each party upon evidence submitted.

As of July 2020, the maximum amount allowed to be taken for a security deposit is five weeks' rent.

The Tenancy Agreement

The most common type of tenancy is an Assured Shorthold Tenancy or AST. These agreements are typically for a minimum of six to twelve months, but can be any length. Tenancies can either be fixed or periodic. Fixed is where both parties are fixed into the contract for an agreed amount of time. A periodic term starts after the fixed term ends on the same terms as the tenancy. This means if rent is paid monthly, each period will be for one month.

These agreements allow a right to tenure (reside) at the property and entitle your right to quiet enjoyment at the property. Quiet enjoyment is a rather generic term, but does legally mean a number of things. This being that a landlord has to provide at least 24 hours' notice if he wishes to visit the property and have a reasonable reason to visit, such as, look at repair work.

An example of an evasion of quiet enjoyment is something I have experienced before. At home with my mum and sisters one evening, we were sitting round the table enjoying our dinner when the landlord, without having provided prior notice of his visit, knocked on the window and asked for some mail that had been mistakenly sent to the property. This happened on a number of occasions.

The landlord would be in breach of contract if a breach of quiet enjoyment got to a level where it became a disruption to your life. In this case you would be able to take legal action.

A tenancy agreement can be written or verbal. For obvious reasons never accept a tenancy agreement without the terms being in writing and being agreed by both parties.

I could write all day about common terms found in tenancy agreements and their implied meaning, but on a general note, ensure that you sit down with a cup of tea and carefully read through each term, picking out anything that doesn't seem right.

Another contractual agreement used for renting residential property can be a licence. This is used for lodgers with live-in landlords.

Ending a tenancy

It is important to keep in mind that when you sign a tenancy you are signing-up for six or 12 months, called the 'fixed term'. The tenancy cannot be ended without the landlord's agreement during the fixed term. If you choose to move out at the end of the fixed term you will need to give two months' written notice.

The other way a tenancy can be ended is during a periodic term. To end a monthly periodic tenancy, you will need to give one month's notice.

The above is the strictly legal way of doing things with the minimum notice periods. In reality, it is a good idea to give your landlord as much notice as possible once you have decided to end the tenancy.

Doing so, will only work in your favour as this will build good relations with the landlord.

If the landlord wants the tenant to move out for any reason, they need to provide a minimum of two months' written notice.

SKILL 28: GETTING A MORTGAGE

It is highly likely at some point in your life you will take out a mortgage. This chapter will give you valuable inside tips to help when selecting a mortgage and dealing with the mortgage broker.

There are good and bad brokers, so do not assume that just because they wear a nice suit, they will get you the best deal, because it may well be the best deal for them. Ask them to refer you to previous clients and please call and ask about their experience.

Also, watch out for fees. Brokers are paid commission by the lender and they must disclose to you how much they are being paid. They may add on a small admin charge, but too much is greedy. Many will not make any charge.

When obtaining a mortgage, the most important thing to keep in mind is that banks only care about two things: firstly, getting their money back; secondly, earning interest. That's it! You need to convince them during the application process that you are good for both, so when you fill-in the paperwork, keep that in mind.

Whenever banks issue a loan, they will always want to take as much 'security' as they can. Security is anything they can use to get their money back should you default on the loan. In the case of mortgages on a home, the security is most commonly the property which is being lent against. Frequently though, if you have other assets they will try to take security over those too, particularly if you are buying through a business. This could be a debenture over company, which is an agreement between you and the bank over all company assets as well as personal guarantees.

There are two main types of mortgage as discussed below:

Capital Repayment

The monthly payments on a repayment mortgage are much more than those on an interest-only mortgage because you are paying both interest and a percentage of the capital. All lenders offer these types of loans.

At the end of the term the mortgage is paid off and you will own the property outright.

Banks will usually only offer a capital repayment mortgage for buying your home. This is the safest type of loan from the bank's perspective because part of the monthly payment is the actual loan amount and part is interest. By the end of the term the mortgage is settled and the loan is repaid.

Some banks play around with the percentages of capital and interest you pay back during the mortgage term. Usually front loading the interest to make sure they squeeze as much interest as possible out of you, should you decide to refinance the property. Ask that question of the broker, "how are the payments made up?".

Interest-only

I always prefer this type of mortgage as the repayments are considerably cheaper. In fact, I would not consider any other type of mortgage.

This type of mortgage is most commonly used for investment property, but can be used to buy your home if you have a deposit of

50% or over. I would strongly suggest you get an interest-only as soon as you can. It means that while you are on this earth, you can enjoy a much better home for much less repayment.

As the name suggests, this type of loan involves paying the interest only on the loan amount each month for the term of the loan. Then at the end of the term, the capital must be repaid.

You hear people say, "oh but I'll never own my home". Who cares? In reality you don't anyway, you are only borrowing it while you are on this earth. In 25 years the house would have gone up in price so much, that you can easily refinance and pay back the capital at that time. I don't know any investors who would even consider a repayment mortgage. It will just make the bank rich quicker and you poorer.

Banks view interest-only as more risk as no capital is being paid off until the end of the term, but boy do they make up for that risk with a whopping 50% deposit requirement.

In the case of investment property, before the bank offers you a mortgage, they will carry out what are called, 'rental stress tests'. This involves testing the borrower's capability to make the interest payments from the rent received, if interest rates were to rise to around 5.5%. This varies from bank to bank.

Typically, with an interest-only loan, you will get an initial fixed term period on a lower interest rate, generally two to five years. Then once the initial fixed term is over, the loan will revert to a higher interest rate which can be quite a bit higher and more expensive. At the end of the fixed term it is common practice to re-mortgage. Using the new mortgage to pay off the old mortgage and being reset on a lower fixed rate again.

The hidden purpose of this is that the bank and the broker gets fees every time you re-mortgage, but it's all part of the game.

Sometimes with interest-only mortgages there are variable rates. This simply means that they track the country's bank base interest rate at a certain percentage above or below that rate. If the base rate for the country changes, so does the variable rate. These are risky for the borrower but can sometimes work out cheaper if interest rates are very low, like they have been for several years now.

Something to be mindful of with interest-only is that at the end of the mortgage term, the principal is still due. But this is often not a problem, as, for example, on a mortgage term of say 25 years, the house will have more than doubled in value and either selling or re-mortgaging the property will pay off the old mortgage.

Applying for a mortgage

When applying for a mortgage you can either go direct to a bank, or more usually go to a broker. I would always advise approaching a broker in the first instance just to see what kind of mortgage products are available as the rates change all the time. Most independent brokers are 'whole of market', meaning they can access lenders across the market. In reality, I've found they have their favourites, those that pay them higher fees, so be careful.

Banks have their own in-house brokers. These only have access to that particular bank's products rather than the whole market, but in some cases the deals can be just as good.

- Sometimes the estate agent you are buying through recommends their in-house mortgage broker and they can sometimes put pressure on you to come and see their broker before they will put forward your offer.

They do this for three reasons. One, they get commission from the broker if you buy through them, and two, they feel they have more control over the purchase, as their broker will communicate your financial position and the progress of the sale to them. Thirdly, it shows the agent that you can afford the property. It's not ethical, but it happens all the time.

Brokers can be biased towards banks who pay them the most commission or push mortgage applications through quickly. This may not be such a bad thing, but make sure they are not charging you a fee on top.

Valuations

Before lending, banks will instruct a valuation to be carried out on the property. This is to check the property is worth the amount you told the broker. Also, that if you defaulted on the loan, the bank would easily be able to sell your property and recoup their money. A certified surveyor will carry out the valuation and compile a report for the bank with their opinion of the value of the property.

These bank valuations nearly always value the property under what you feel it is worth. The bank-nominated surveyors do this on purpose to give the bank more margin in the house if they have to sell due to your default.

It is important to note this is just a financial valuation for the bank and is nothing to do with the condition of the property. If you feel there is something wrong with the property you may instruct a homebuyers' survey or even a full structural survey for your own peace of mind. Any defects found can be the subject of price negotiations.

Loan to value (LTV)

The LTV is the loan amount against the value of the property. If a property is worth £100k and the loan is £75k, the LTV will be 75%. The higher the LTV, the lower deposit amount needed.

When buying your personal home, the highest LTV you will get at the moment will generally be 75%, although this does depend on your situation, age and the individual lender.

Occasionally the government will announce a particular short-term deal for property buyers. At present, there is a stamp-duty holiday which is banded depending on the value of the property you are buying. Also, the mortgage guarantee scheme, which allows you to buy property at a LTV up to 95%. But these are short-term schemes and you should always be advised by your mortgage broker.

When buying an investment property, the highest is generally also 75% at the time of writing.

Mortgage Underwriting

Mortgage underwriting after the property crash of 2008 has been taken to new levels. The bank will conduct a deep dive into your financial situation and it is a good idea to be ready for any documentation they may request and to have your house in order when starting this process. Banks will run a credit check on you so it is highly beneficial to have a clean credit score. See Skill 29.

Banks view self-employed persons as riskier and sometimes will not offer as high an LTV as a result.

As long as you keep in mind banks' number one rule during this process you should be fine; banks want their money back and they want interest.

SKILL 29: LOANS & CREDIT SCORES

What is a credit

Credit is the foundation of the capitalist system itself, it oils the wheels of business and enables our economy to grow. Credit enables people with ideas but no money the opportunity to fulfil their dreams. If no one were willing to finance other people's ventures, entrepreneurialism would come to a halt.

When you apply for a loan the lender will assess you as a borrower against their lending criteria. This is a tick box exercise which is to assess the likelihood of you paying their loan back. A big part of their criteria will be your credit score.

Credit is when an institution (or anyone) agrees to lend money to a borrower over a set period of time on agreed terms and there is always interest to pay. Apart from some 0% car deals.

It's fairly easy to apply for a loan, just fill out the necessary forms and submit them to the lender. The degree to which you will be successful will depend to a very large degree on your credit score. Therefore, it's very important that you understand how the credit score system works to protect your financial future.

Credit score

A credit score has become the universally accepted tool used by lenders to help them determine whether you qualify for a particular loan, be it credit card, car loan, mobile phone contract, mortgage or other loan.

There are three main credit rating agencies in the UK, Equifax. Experian and TransUnion. These are private companies who act as information brokers between you and the organisation you have applied to for credit. They earn their money by selling your information to these companies, and also by subscriptions from the public.

Experian, for example, charge £14.99 per month following a 30-day trial, which gives you instant access to your credit report. Not many people know that by law credit agencies must also provide you with one free credit report annually, but only if you request a copy.

I want to make an important point. I can't stress enough the importance of having a good credit score. Having a bad score can really disrupt your life. I learned this the hard way.

In my early twenties, my bank asked me if I wanted a credit card, which cost around £13 a year. I'd never had a credit card so said yes. The card arrived and I threw it in a drawer until I eventually lost it when I moved house.

Many years later I tried to get a mortgage and was refused. I couldn't understand why, I ran a successful business, owned my own home and had no debt at all. I asked my mortgage broker to speak to the lender and they said I had a County Court Judgement CCJ against me for £135 and that no one would lend me money.

I told my broker I'd never had any negative financial issues, there must be some mistake. He said there wasn't and I did have a CCJ against my name in favour of Barclays Bank for non-payment of £135. It still didn't click, but when I asked my bank manager to look into it for me, he told me it was for non-payment of a credit card fee I'd taken out years ago.

To cut a very long story short, it turned out that Barclays, the issuer of the card, had sent me a bill every year for £13. The problem was that I'd moved-house and not changed my address at the bank. All the letters were going to my old address and eventually, when I didn't reply, Barclays took legal action against me and sent those letters to my old address too. I was found guilty without even knowing I was being sued. Pretty unbelievable, but it meant I couldn't buy a car or house, no credit at all.

It affected my business and personal life massively and I lost the house we wanted, so I wasn't popular with the other half either.

I haven't time here to go into the months and months of letters, phone calls and emails that it took to sort it out, but I can say that it was a very stressful issue to deal with.

So please, don't brush this issue under the carpet, look after your credit score.

How credit scores work

Credit agencies build a credit report on you. Using that information, credit agencies calculate a numerical score that represents your credit history. This helps to indicate what kind of borrower you are and how likely it is that you will manage your repayments.

Where do agencies get your information from?

Credit agencies get information from the organisations you owe money to, called your creditors, such as banks, credit card issuers or car finance companies. They also get information from public records such as property or court records.

Is a high credit score better than a low one?

The higher your score the better. Higher scores mean lenders see you as less risk and they will often offer you more money.

Experian, for example, see a good score to be between 881 and 960, a fair score between 721 and 880, with 999 being the top score.

It's worth remembering that lenders vary in the way they work out credit scores, so if you don't meet the criteria of one lender, you may still be able to get credit with another.

If you are refused credit at any time, the most important thing is to find out why. Then rectify the problem before applying again. Do not do nothing.

Frequency of searches

Something that caught me out years ago was the high number of searches that banks were taking out on me. I was building my property portfolio and buying multiple properties in quick succession. Unbeknown to me, if there are several searches against you in a short period of time, this is a negative against your credit score.

While this is the case for mortgages, it is not the case for cars. Credit agencies expect you to shop around for prices with different dealers and this is seen as a positive. Therefore, all enquiries for car loans within a given period of time, usually around 14 days, counts as a single inquiry. There is no sense to it, but that's how it is.

These are called hard or soft enquiries. A hard enquiry is shown on your report, a soft enquiry isn't. It's very important that you find out whether the enquiry for what you are about to buy, will show up on your report.

How does a young person get credit?

The issue young people have is that they have no credit history. Therefore, lenders have nothing to access your loan application against. It's important that you get going and build a credit history as soon as possible.

Some things you could do are as follows:

- Take out a credit card in your name.
- Ask a parent to add you to one of their credit cards. But only if they pay their bills on time. I'm not a fan of credit cards, but here they serve a purpose.

Reasons to build a credit score

In short, any borrowing, be it for renting a flat, mobile phone contract, buying a house or car, will require a good credit score. You are very restricted financially with a bad score, especially if you run a business.

How long does negative information stay on your credit report?

Seven years is the norm. The one major exception being bankruptcies, which can stay on your credit reports for ten years.

Things to avoid

The key here is to keep your finances organised (Skill 30) and to know every outgoing and incoming. Keep on top of monthly payments and cancel any DDs or SOs you no longer need. Things to avoid are:

- Taking on too much debt.
- Too much credit card debt (always pay at least a third of the monthly balance).
- Forgetting to close accounts.
- Forgetting to pay off utility bills when you move out of rental property or move home.
- Paying off old phone contracts if you switch accounts.
- Submitting too many loan applications.
- Forgetting to register on the electoral roll (Biggie).

These will all negatively affect your credit rating.

In conclusion, and at risk of repeating myself, get on-top of your finances and check your credit score regularly.

SKILL 30:
ORGANISING YOUR FINANCES

For many years my idea of money management was going to the cash point and pressing the 'check balance' button. Either I had money or I didn't. But at that time my life mainly consisted of being paid every month and spending all that on clothes and partying.

As I got older my finances became more complicated. I'd taken on a car loan, motorbike loan and mortgage. I had utility bills, council tax, income tax and a TV licence. Plus, the cost of bringing up five sons. I won't even go down that road. One income but with many outgoings. It could have got very confusing and needless to say, that if I'd not kept a close eye on my finances I could have let a lot of people down and my credit score could have suffered.

The method I use now is very similar to that which I use in our businesses, a simple profit and loss statement, P&L.

It's a good idea to make this very detailed. Write all your expenses in one column and your incomings – for most of you your wage – in the other.

In your expenses column write the name of the company or person you are paying, so you can match this up with your bank statement. That way you can be sure the company the money has gone to is the same as the name on your P&L.

You can see from the example below that's it's very simple and easy to update straight from your bank statements.

One evening's work and you've gone from sleepless nights worrying if you've got enough money to get to the end of the month, to organised and in control.

You should check your P&L regularly and I can assure you that when you do you end up feeling very in control.

Get into this habit early in life and keep it all the way through life, and it will serve you well.

One last thing to mention. Under expenses, the top of the list will obviously be savings, will it not?

INCOME AND EXPENSE SHEET			
Income	Monthly	Yearly	
Net Salary	£2,200.00	£26,400.00	
Outgoings			
Rent	£515.00	£6,180.00	
Home Running Costs			
Council Tax	£98.00	£1,176.00	
Phones BT (Sky + Broadband)	£42.00	£504.00	
TV Licence	£12.37	£148.44	
Water	£38.00	£456.00	
Water sewerage	£12.00	£144.00	
Electricity and Gas	£121.00	£1,452.00	
Mobile	£25.00	£300.00	
Home Insurances	£25.00	£300.00	
Total	£373.37	£4,480.44	17.0%
Living Costs			
Food	£230.00	£2,760.00	
Christmas & Birthdays	£80.00	£960.00	

Hair/Nails	£20.00	£240.00	
Contact lenses	£18.00	£216.00	
Clothes	£25.00	£300.00	
Total	£373.00	£4,476.00	17.0%
Leisure			
Eating Out – Coffee Shops –– Social	£80.00	£960.00	
Holidays	£200.00	£2,400.00	
Total	£280.00	£3,360.00	12.7%
Cars			
Car Loan	£190.00	£2,280.00	
Car Insurance	£28.00	£336.00	
Petrol	£65.00	£780.00	
Total	£283.00	£3,396.00	12.9%
Education			
Audible and Books	£35.00	£420.00	1.6%
Total Outgoing	£1,859.37	£22,312.44	
Possible Savings	£340.63	£4,087.56	15.5%

AFTERWORD

As my knowledge and experience have improved, I've improved as a parent and I've been able to pass on better knowledge to my five sons.

When I was a young man, my three elder sons got the no-nonsense business man. Later in life, the two younger boys got the shrewd investor dad. All of my sons are doing very well, but it has to be said that the younger two will probably be financially free earlier than the others.

I have seen first-hand the astonishing things that can be achieved by such young people who understand the Skills in this book and are willing to take action on them. I hope they will do the same for you.

This is why I wrote the book.

Alex, my youngest son, told me recently he feels sad every time he does a credit check on someone. I asked him why. He said he felt sorry for the people applying to rent our properties, as most of them live day-to-day financially and many could not even pass the credit check. He said it made him feel sad and very lucky.

This is another reason I wrote this book.

I am not suggesting money is everything, because it is not. One of my favourite pastimes is walking up mountains and that doesn't cost a penny. But walking in the French Alps with the safest walking gear, on the other hand, does cost money. This is the point. Money itself does not make you happy. It enables you to do the finer things in life and moreover allows you the free time to do those things with the ones you love.

To me this is worth working hard for in your younger life.

Sadly, because of the fraudulent banking system, many young people today can't afford a mortgage and are having to live with their parents way longer than they may want.

The simple truth is, if you live your life as a consumer with an average job, the chances are you are going to struggle with money. But, if you follow the path I've laid out for you in this book, even if you are a low-income earner, you can still achieve financial freedom.

The choice is yours.

The knowledge in this book won't change your circumstances at all. Taking action on that knowledge definitely will. One won't work without the other.

I said in my introduction that this book is for you if you want to become wealthy. I have proven to you in Skill 16 with a clear formula that anyone with enough skill and determination who takes the required action can become wealthy. I've given you the skills, now it's up to you provide the determination and take the action.

I have summarised the main actions for you here:

- Have a great attitude at work. Be the most helpful worker in the firm and ask for a pay rise.
- Be obsessive about saving money while you are young.
- Learn all you can about money and investing.
- Limit the number of liabilities you buy. Keep away from expensive cars.
- Buy mostly the things you 'need' rather than 'want'.
- Pay yourself first.

- Buy appreciating assets as soon as you have saved enough money.
- Save again and repeat the process until you reach the amount of passive income you are happy with.
- Don't listen to the naysayers.

Lastly, it just remains for me to wish you the very best on your journey.

Please believe YOU CAN DO IT; you can do anything you put your mind to.

Good luck!

Ray Spooner.

Other Books by the Author

50 Skills – The Entrepreneurs' Handbook

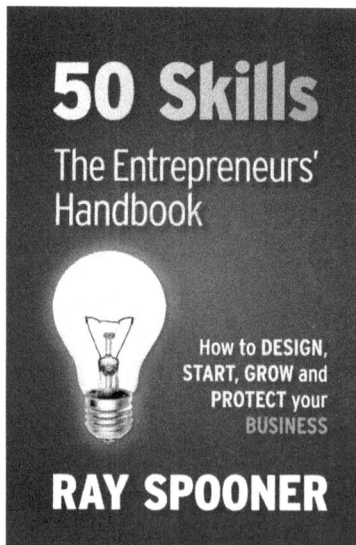

www.ingramcontent.com/pod-product-compliance
Lightning Source LLC
Chambersburg PA
CBHW071700200326
41519CB00012BA/2578